Jeanne Guyon's Christian Worldview

Jeanne Guyon's Christian Worldview

Her Biblical Commentaries on Galatians, Ephesians,
and Colossians with Explanations and Reflections
on the Interior Life

By
JEANNE DE LA MOTHE GUYON

Introduction and Translation from the Original French
by Nancy Carol James

Foreword by William Bradley Roberts

PICKWICK *Publications* · Eugene, Oregon

JEANNE GUYON'S CHRISTIAN WORLDVIEW
Her Biblical Commentaries on Galatians, Ephesians, and Colossians with Explanations and Reflections on the Interior Life

Pickwick Publications
An Imprint of Wipf and Stock Publishers
199 W. 8th Ave., Suite 3
Eugene, OR 97401

www.wipfandstock.com

PAPERBACK ISBN: 978-1-5326-0498-0
HARDCOVER ISBN: 978-1-5326-0500-0
EBOOK ISBN: 978-1-5326-0499-7

Cataloguing-in-Publication data:

Names: Guyon, Jeanne Marie Bouvier de La Motte, 1648–1717 | James, Nancy C., 1954–, translator | Roberts, William Bradley, foreword writer

Title: Jeanne Guyon's Christian worldview : her biblical commentaries on Galatians, Ephesians, and Colossians with explanations and reflections on the interior life / Jeanne Guyon, translated by Nancy Carol James.

Description: Eugene, OR: Pickwick Publications, 2017 | Includes bibliographical references.

Identifiers: ISBN 978-1-5326-0498-0 (paperback) | ISBN 978-1-5326-0500-0 (hardcover) | ISBN 978-1-5326-0499-7 (ebook)

Subjects: LCSH: Guyon, Jeanne Marie Bouvier de La Motte, 1648–1717 | Bible. Galatians—Commentaries | Bible. Ephesians—Commentaries | Bible. Colossians—Commentaries | Quietism

Classification: BX4705.G8 G891 2017 (paperback) | BX4705.G8 (ebook)

Manufactured in the U.S.A.   10/31/17

Dedicated to Roger James Nebel

Contents

Foreword

FROM HER RIVETING BOOK *Standing in the Whirlwind,* one discovers something of the harrowing details of Nancy James's early ministry as an Episcopal priest.[1] She learned first-hand that a faithful life entails suffering. Reading that memoir sheds light on why James might have been drawn to Guyon. This deeply faithful seventeenth-/eighteenth-century woman was subjected to grievous mistreatment at the hands of civil and religious authorities, including several years of imprisonment. Guyon's voice is still prophetic today. While despots cling desperately to their authority, the prophet's authority arises from integrity.

This volume is James's tenth book on Madame Guyon, placing James clearly in the forefront of Guyon scholarship. One senses James's ever-deepening wisdom in these cumulative studies, each new book building on the achievements of the last.

As with all effective translations, James's rendering of Guyon reads as if English were the original language. No awkward syntax, clumsy constructions, or questionable word choices litter James's treatment of Guyon's text. It reads smoothly. Anyone who has attempted translating will attest that such a natural flow of language does not appear on its own, but is instead the result of meticulous work, trying this word and that, until the new language is as fluid as the original.

When Guyon labels her work "A prayerful guide" she lays bare her motive for writing it. She wants to impart the deep wisdom she has discovered in these three biblical letters. To call this "a devotional book" implies no condescension. If Guyon's book were only a scholarly study, the reader

---

1. James, *Standing in the Whirlwind.*

would not encounter a phrase like, "O wonderful truth! How is it that all Christians do not comprehend this point?"[2]

The reader cannot understand Guyon or her writing without accepting Guyon's passion. Indeed, passion is probably the most compelling aspect of these commentaries.

James finds no occasion for embarrassment in Guyon's flights of spiritual ecstasy, but instead allows her to speak richly in her own voice. As a result, that voice comes across as precise and clear as if the reader were visiting with Guyon in her own time.

Galatians scholar J. Louis Martyn says that reading Paul's letter to the Galatian churches is "like coming in on a play as the curtain is rising on the third or fourth act."[3] The plot is already thick, demonstrated in the opening lines, which tell us three things: 1) There is high drama here, because of the deep love and angry tension between Paul and this church. 2) There is a rich history between the Galatians and Paul. 3) A number of actors besides Paul and the Galatians have already appeared on stage, and understanding the book involves knowing their roles.

Guyon understands this drama intuitively, and responds to the text as if she knows the actors. Galatians 2:20 says, "It is no longer I who live, but it is Christ who lives in me. And the life I now live in the flesh I live by faith in the Son of God, who loved me and gave himself for me." Guyon responds: "Now I live by faith in the Son of God. Jesus Christ lives in me and it is He who works in me. Jesus Christ leads and governs me. His life is my life. His Spirit communicates with me. He fills my soul with His Spirit and life. Therefore, I see nothing within or without except Jesus Christ who lives within me."[4] Guyon quotes the biblical texts in brief portions, then delves headlong into their meaning and application to daily life. Like the writers of the epistles, her life is centered in the person of Jesus, and this resonates in her testimony.

Accepting an authentic Pauline authorship of Ephesians (disputed among some scholars), and assuming that Paul was martyred in Rome in AD 63, then the letter was written in Rome in the years 61–63. If written in Caesarea, then the date is two or three years earlier.[5]

---

2. Guyon, *Commentaries*, 46.

3. Martyn, *Galatians*, 13.

4. Guyon, *Commentaries*, 34.

5. Barth, *Ephesians*, 51.

Since Guyon begins with the assumption of Pauline authorship, one wants to read her book from that perspective.

We know little about the setting or date of Paul's letter to the Colossians. What theological and practical matters gave rise to it? We can only speculate. The biblical book, nevertheless, contributes much to understanding Paul's mind and pastoral ministry, and this makes Colossians fascinating reading. The letter presents the person of Jesus Christ as the answer to human questions about the cosmos.[6]

It is no wonder, then, that Madame Guyon was drawn to comment on Colossians, because her life was grounded in her relationship with Jesus. As she writes, we quickly begin to understand her utter devotion to Jesus as the source of wisdom and guidance.

In her commentary on these three biblical books, Guyon ushers us into her understanding of Scripture as rooted in a mystical relationship with God. The reader not only is instructed by Madame Guyon in matters spiritual but also enters into an intimate conversation about life in Christ. We witness her courage in bold responses to Scripture, applying it to everyday life for the believer.

Readers will find in this volume a source of knowledge and inspiration. One cannot help but be moved by Guyon's direct, heart-centered, and passionate talk about living life with God as one's companion. James's rich translation of Guyon might indeed yield more spiritual companions.

The Rev. William Bradley Roberts, DMA.
Professor Church Music and Director of Chapel Music
Virginia Theological Seminary
Alexandria, VA
February 3, 2017

---

6. Martin, *Ephesians*, 81.

Preface

WHEN IN GRADUATE SCHOOL at the University of Virginia, I searched using the phrase "religious mysticism" and the computer screen showed the author Madame Guyon. I wondered who she was and found her book *The Autobiography of Madame Guyon.* I opened and read the testimony of Guyon's life. Since that first time of reading Jeanne Guyon's theology, my life has continually been deepened and enriched by Guyon's Christian worldview.

I offer this volume to those who study her and those wishing to live the profound Christian faith.

These are the first English translation of Guyon's French commentaries of the letters of the Galatians, Ephesians, and Colossians. I translated these commentaries after I realized that here she expressed the essence of her Christian theology. Guyon studied specific verses from Galatians, Ephesians, and Colossians and wrote her ideas about them. Guyon developed her theology about the interior life based on these letters.

Guyon chose to write only about certain verses from these letters. She also did not repeat herself and covered ideas only once. This translation mirrors the original French commentary with integrity. Also, Guyon treasured the idea that Christ is the bridegroom of the soul and used male pronouns for God and female pronouns for the soul and the person. I have used her method and so throughout this volume female pronouns are employed for the reference to a person and male for God and Christ.

For the Bible translation, I chose the New Revised Standard Version.

Acknowledgments

Many people have contributed to this volume. I am grateful for the support of Dr. Carlos Eire during my dissertation work on Jeanne Guyon. I thank Rev. William Roberts for his understanding of Jeanne Guyon's theology and his foreword, which makes a substantial contribution to this book.

I want to thank the parishioners of St. John's, Lafayette Square, Washington DC for their dialogue about Jeanne Guyon and her rich theology.

Many thanks go to my family who shares my passion for the work of Jeanne Guyon. Roger, Hannah, and Melora have read, explored, and researched Jeanne Guyon along with me. I am grateful that we share this love.

Above all, I thank my readers who share a love for Jeanne Guyon and her ideas about the Christian life. Guyon's books have been kept alive by those who continue to seek a profound interior live lived with Christ. I hope that Guyon's Christian worldview lives for centuries yet to come.

Introduction

In about 34 AD, the Pharisee named Saul furiously thundered on horseback toward Damascus with legal orders to arrest and kill Christians. A great light knocked Paul off of his horse and he heard the words "Saul, Saul, why do you persecute me?" He asked, "Who are you, Lord?" The reply came, "I am Jesus, whom you are persecuting. But get up and enter the city, and you will be told what you are to do" (Acts 9:4–6). After this experience, Saul (his name later changed to Paul) found grace to know and love Jesus Christ, the Son of God.

In France in 1664, the fifteen-year-old Jeanne Guyon was forced into an arranged and unhappy marriage with an older man. In 1668 when pregnant with her second child, Jeanne, tempted by thoughts of suicide and despair, sought spiritual counsel from a monk. He told her that she could find God within her heart and immediately she felt Christ filling her with love. She wrote about this saying, "O my Lord, you were in my heart and you asked from me only a simple turning inward to make me feel your presence. O infinite Goodness, you were so near."[7]

These two encounters with the risen Jesus Christ led to this book. Paul discovered the reality of Jesus Christ's gift of grace. Between 57 and 63 AD, Paul wrote letters to churches in Galatia, Ephesus, and Colossae discussing the life lived with Christ. Centuries later, Guyon discovered the same truth of the risen Christ. In the late 1600s, Guyon studied Paul's letters and wrote commentaries on his ideas to help readers understand the good news. She

---

7. James, *Pure Love*, 27.

described how Paul lived his life in complete trust and dependence on Jesus Christ and how other believers are to do the same. Guyon wrote about these letters with passion, describing this life with hope. Guyon writes, "God is pleased to remake us in his image by his Word by inviting us to live within him. O, adorable grandeur! O, the wonderful marvel that we discover in our interior! We receive this wisdom by dwelling within you!"[8]

In his lifetime Paul had his faith tested in his many afflictions and incarcerations, as later did Guyon. Yet both testified that the Lord's presence cared for them in the midst of their suffering, bringing them peace and joy even in the midst of persecutions.

Jeanne Guyon's biblical commentaries on Paul's letters of Galatians, Ephesians, and Colossians have never been translated into English. I present these first English translations for scholars who are researching and studying the ideas of Jeanne Guyon, as well as for those seeking a more profound knowledge of Jesus Christ.

JEANNE GUYON'S LIFE (1648–1717)

Born into an aristocratic family in France, Jeanne de la Mothe grew up in the town of Montargis on the Loire River. Both of her parents had been married before and their blended family experienced constant tensions and arguments. In the midst of this unhappiness, the mother preferred certain of her children and neglected Guyon. As a young teenager, Guyon's parents forced her into an arranged marriage to Jacques Guyon, a wealthy man twenty-two years older than she. This mismatched couple had many conflicts and she became miserable. By the age of nineteen and pregnant with her second child, Guyon experienced a crisis in which she could not endure her life anymore. She spoke to a Franciscan monk, Father Archange Enguerrand, who counseled her that God's wisdom was inside of her. He told her, "It is, Madame, because you seek without what you have within. Accustom yourself to seek God in your heart, and you will find God there."[9] Guyon wrote that she felt relief from the sudden presence of God within her heart.

Following this revelation, Guyon committed herself to Christ. Against the wishes of her husband, she chose a small closet in her home and prayed there regularly. She also worked raising her five children, instead of giving

8. Guyon, *Commentaries*, 70.

9. Guyon, *Complete Madame Guyon*, 8.

this responsibility to their servants. When a smallpox epidemic hit, two of her children died. Yet even in the midst of sorrows, Guyon's faith grew. She threw herself into ministering in the villages among the poor. She knew some peace with her husband, although the relationship continued to be a difficult one. She also began to write her ideas about the Christian faith. Whenever she had time, Guyon grabbed pen and paper and captured her ideas about God. She wrote about her love for God, "I loved him, and I burned with his fire because I loved him, and I loved him in such a way that I could love only him, but in loving him I had no motive save himself."[10]

In 1676 her husband died when she was twenty-eight, leaving her a wealthy widow with two older sons and a small daughter. Guyon said she would never marry again and moved to a small town outside of Geneva. She chose a quiet life living in rural cottages with her young daughter. There Guyon intensified her active ministry with the sick and wrote continually. She frequently spent all night working on her books, saying that the ideas sparked by the Bible flowed quickly on to paper. She spent her time searching the scriptures, praying and looking for answers about Christ's relationship with her. With the help of a friend, she published her books and they quickly found great popularity throughout Europe. Her better known books include her *Autobiography, The Short and Easy Method of Prayer*, and *Spiritual Torrents*.

Then Guyon faced serious persecution about her Christian writing, including accusations from church leaders that a woman should not even write. The tensions in her childhood family surfaced again when her half-brother betrayed her to the Roman Catholic powers of the Inquisition and accused her of immorality. Church and state authorities arrested and incarcerated her.

With Guyon's aristocratic connections to Louis XIV's court at Versailles, some leaders spoke out, protesting the treatment of this gentle woman. The tutor for King Louis's grandson, Archbishop François Fénelon, courageously defended Guyon and declared her innocent. Because of this, King Louis XIV banished Fénelon from his court and in 1697 reported him to Rome as writing heretical books. The king's actions publicized this controversy throughout Europe and heightened the political conflicts surrounding Guyon's incarceration. The cardinals in Rome debated the orthodoxy of Fénelon's book about Guyon's theology called *The Maxims of the Saints*. Many in state and church position in Europe watched this situation

---

10. James, *Pure Love*, 18.

and it became called "The Great Conflict." In 1699 Pope Innocent XII censured twenty-three propositions of Fénelon's book.

While this was happening, Guyon endured many brutal twelve-hour interrogations. Authorities searched for evidence of any type of wrongdoing and would free her only to arrest her again. At the instigation of Bishop Jacques Bénigne Bossuet, preacher to King Louis XIV, she suffered several incarcerations, including an incarceration in the Bastille from 1698–1703. Guyon spent a total of about ten years incarcerated in four different places of imprisonment.

During these years of forced solitude, Guyon continued to pray and wrote that her interior faith carried her through these years of persecutions. Finally, Bishop Bossuet exonerated her of all charges. Following this, Guyon was released from the Bastille and lived for fourteen years in a cottage in Blois near her daughter's residence. During her final years, she gave spiritual counsel to many Catholics, Quakers and Protestants, both in meetings and letters.

More about Guyon's life is written in *The Pure Love of Madame Guyon: The Great Conflict in King Louis XIV's Court*.[11]

JEANNE GUYON'S INTERIOR FAITH

Jeanne Guyon, a woman despised and hated by many in seventeenth-century France, dedicated herself to Jesus Christ and to living the Christian interior life. She offered her commentaries on the Bible as help in the search for the interior kingdom of God. With a profound clarity of thought, she understood the gospel message of the redemptive work accomplished by the life, passion, and crucifixion of Jesus Christ as the central focus of both the Old and New Testaments.

Guyon's hidden treasure of thought needs to be seen as the extraordinary accomplishment it is: one woman, persecuted and incarcerated, explained the complete biblical message to readers. Basing her ideas on the words of Jesus, she says that our greatest longing is for the pure love of God. Christ tells us, "Love the Lord your God with all your heart, mind, strength and soul" (Luke 10:27). Guyon's thinking is simple: If Christ commands us to do this, then how can this be an impossibility? Christ commands us and by his rich and generous grace he gives us the ability and power to do this.

---

11. Ibid.

Guyon described the beginning of this spiritual life as surrender to Christ. The believer then learns to love Christ with purity and finds fulfillment in participating in Christ. From this interior encounter with Christ, believers learn to live in a way pleasing to God. Using this Scripture of Luke 10:27, she defined the interior life as that of the heart, mind, strength, and soul. Guyon explains to us how a faithful person may answer Christ's call to love him with all of our heart, mind, strength, and soul, which means, in brief, to love him with our interior life.

Guyon called this encounter with the living Lord the interior life. Christians find the great mystery that Christ lives within us, and in trusting and receiving Christ, live in the midst of the Trinity in the love springing forth among the Father and the Son and Holy Spirit. Truly, divine love surrounds believers and unites them with the Holy Trinity.

Guyon applied this wisdom from the interior life to her defense against the inquisition by the Roman Catholic Church. With no formal education, Guyon came up against the most educated church leaders of the time. Guyon was not allowed to have a lawyer in the interrogations and she said that God within gave her the words to say. In many court interrogations, Guyon told officials that the pure love of God should rule our interior life. Her answers in the interrogations finally led to her judgment of innocent. The many officials that investigated her could find no wrong doing in her life or thinking.

Yet even with all the suffering, Guyon remained peaceful. She says that the Lord calls us to enjoy him. In her *Commentary on Ephesians*, she writes, "This enjoyment underlies all of our experience, as if we were given a taste for an exquisite thing that was promised to us; to desire this is a great advantage." Our enjoyment of the Lord grows into a powerful relationship with Jesus Christ. She continues, "In Jesus Christ, human beings become the inheritance of God, as God wants to be the inheritance of human beings."[12]

Guyon went on to emphasize the believer's enjoyment of the whole Trinity. The mystery she sought to explain is that that the Son mediates the immense reality of the Trinity to the faithful person. Guyon describes, "The Son contains the profundity and immensity of the Trinity because Jesus Christ is the breadth and length and height and depth of the Father." The invitation for the faithful is to live in and unite with the Trinity. The infinite Trinity holds and supports the believer while inviting the person to enjoy the revelation of the glory of Christ and participate in the profound depths

---

12. Guyon, *Commentaries*, 79–80.

of wisdom that God the Father offers the believer. In brief, the love that emanates and flows between each member of the Trinity flows upon and within the believer in a continual expression of love.

The mystery is that Jesus Christ forms himself in the believer's interior life. In her *Commentary on Colossians*, Guyon writes, "This Gospel tells us the truth of the wonderful mystery, that is, Christ came to live within us . . . We need to comprehend the truth of his living within us and to be assured by this."[13]

THE CHRISTIAN WORLDVIEW OF JEANNE GUYON

The essence of the Christian worldview is this revelation and manifestation of Jesus Christ as the Son of God within the heart, mind, and soul of the believer. In Guyon's Christian worldview, the heart of Jesus Christ graciously offers salvation, as he accomplishes the mystery of the redemption of humanity. Jesus Christ lives within the believer's interior life.

Guyon sought to understand the Christian worldview in her prayerful study of the Bible. In her biblical commentaries, Guyon structured her writing by writing out a few verses from Paul's letters and then writing some paragraphs about the meaning of these verses. She looked to the Apostle Paul for wisdom about the interior life because he too sought a living relationship with Jesus Christ. In these letters, Paul describes both the richness of this life and the temptations that happen on the way. He lists the actions that flow naturally out of the Christian interior life.

Throughout her writings, Guyon summarizes her ideas about the believer's Christian worldview. Guyon described her ideas about the spiritual life and wrote about this from her personal perspective (writing with the pronouns "I" and "we") based on Paul's witness in these epistles. According to Guyon, we can find a path to God, our Beloved.

Guyon describes this relationship with God in simplicity. The interior life begins with surrender to the living Lord. People see no path to God the Father and realize the truth that there is no path without Jesus Christ. God has sent us his only Son so by the great mystery of revelation, Jesus Christ becomes real to us. All of our powers, heart, and mind become strengthened when we see the Lord with eyes of faith. Jesus Christ calls to us and asks us to give him everything. In a wave of faith, we answer Christ, saying, "Yes!" to him and accepting our completion in him. We hear his wisdom,

13 Ibid., 81–82.

experience his healing, and feel his gracious kindness. We cling to him in utter dependency. We look to him to meet all of our needs.

As we do this, Guyon says we find a new and growing interior life within our heart, mind, strength, and soul that opens up a living place of encounter with Christ. In prayer we welcome Christ's wisdom and salvation inside. We see that he offers to us a large and gracious interior kingdom where we revel in the Word of God. We accept the Scriptures and let them soak into our soul. We learn to love the Lord our God with our heart, mind, strength, and soul.

Following this, our lives become a place of Christ's work. We learn to look eagerly for Christ's presence. Surrendering and yielding to Christ's power, he pours new virtues within us: love, faith, and hope are some of the first to open our interior life. As a believer loves Christ and develops an interior relationship, she begins to transform into becoming more like Christ and brings Christ more into the world. The believer lives Christ within her heart, mind, and soul and then bears the marks of Jesus Christ in the exterior life.

The revelation of this mystery of Jesus Christ, the Son of God, is the point of Paul's letters to the Galatians, Ephesians, and Colossians. Our interior relationship with Jesus Christ is the great mystery revealed to each of us. Guyon writes at the end of her *Commentary on Ephesians*, "Paul wrote this epistle that God gave him in prison, so that through all the centuries we would be instructed by it . . . The person, who has faith and love, also has peace. Paul desires that grace be unto all who have an undying love for Jesus Christ. This grace of graces and the source of all graces is pure love: without it all the other graces are not graces. God gives purity and he gives us pure love."[14]

These commentaries on Galatians, Ephesians, and Colossians describe Jeanne Guyon's Christian worldview. Even in the midst of extreme suffering, she enjoyed the presence of Christ and invites all to this rich and fulfilling life.

The Rev. Nancy Carol James, PhD
January 1, 2017

14. Ibid., 135.

Guyon's *Commentary on Paul's Letter to the Galatians with Explanations and Reflections on the Interior Life*

> Paul—sent neither by human commission nor from human authorities, but through Jesus Christ and God the Father, who raised him from the dead—2 and all the members of God's family who are with me, to the churches of Galatia: 3 Grace to you and peace from God our Father and the Lord Jesus Christ, 4 who gave himself for our sins to set us free from the present evil age, according to the will of our God and Father, 5 to whom be the glory forever and ever. Amen. (Gal 1:1–5)

PAUL TELLS US GOD chooses some ministers and gives them the authority of an apostle. Paul was an apostle of this kind. He was chosen by the resurrected Jesus Christ yet did not know Jesus in this world. Because of this, he did not have the advantage of the other apostles who lived with Jesus Christ.

An apostle has the privilege to communicate grace and peace to those who approach. In fact, the apostle's true character is to communicate peace, because the spirit of Jesus Christ animates an apostle. An apostle must carry peace as Jesus Christ bore it on earth. But to whom did Jesus show himself on earth? To those who received his word and were his disciples, as he spoke to them: "Peace I leave with you; my peace I give to you. I do not give to you as the world gives" (John 14:27).

We know that the world gives only a superficial peace grounded on profound disorder, violence, and war.

Jesus Christ gives his peace only to his followers. He says, "Do not think I have come to bring peace to the earth; I have not come to bring peace, but a sword" (Matt 10:34). His word is peace for us. Others, though, reject Jesus Christ's word and instead choose a sword for their peace. Jesus Christ gives us his peace and delivers us from our sins. By his actions, we are delivered from this evil century, so full of trouble and war. The will of God is that we are delivered and separated from this evil century.

> I am astonished that you are so quickly deserting the one who called you in the grace of Christ and are turning to a different gospel—7 not that there is another gospel, but there are some who are confusing you and want to pervert the gospel of Christ. 8 But even if we or an angel from heaven should proclaim to you a gospel contrary to what we proclaimed to you, let that one be accursed! (Gal 1:6–8)

It is a strange thing to know that even at the birth and beginning of the Christian faith, some people were fighting against the purity of our faith. We know from these Scriptures that the church has been persecuted since its inception. Evil is always actively trying to destroy the church. We know that the devil had tried to destroy Jesus Christ when he was an infant by persuading Herod to kill him. Because of this, Joseph took the infant Jesus to Egypt to save him. Later the devil inspired the crucifixion of Jesus and then these evil powers believed that they had annihilated him by his death. However, Jesus frustrated their plan, because his divine Father resurrected him from the dead. When believers are persecuted, Jesus carries all faithful believers in his heart. We all have victory through the power of Jesus Christ's resurrection.

But the power of evil did not give up when his plans to destroy both Jesus Christ and the beginning of the church failed. The devil saw that he had not been successful in destroying the early church. So he made a plan to deceive the human race. The devil began persecuting Jesus' children. He relentlessly worked to have people kill the faithful Christians. But the devil did not know that the blood of the martyrs is a seed that produces one hundred percent. Instead of destroying the church, these martyrs established the church. The devil's second deception was the one Paul confronts in his letter to the Galatians. The devil deceived people about the law and tried to destroy the pure freedom of the Gospel. He made people believe falsely that they needed to still follow the rigors and details of the law. By going back to the law, these believers desert the gospel.

We know that Jesus Christ wants to give birth to new children in his church by placing his pure spirit within them. Because the Spirit of the Lord is always the same, it is certain that his children live in the purity of the Holy Spirit. Faithful Christians differ from these others who fall into error and derangement designed by the devil. These who fall under the power of evil are soon lost from the Spirit of the Lord, that is to say, they lose the spirit of docility and dependence on the movement of the Holy Spirit.

God wants to establish his faith in all his children and to reunite all the nations under his faith by his Spirit. The jealous devil always fights against the church. He wants the persecution of all Christians and tries to destroy the interior knowledge of the faith that grows within the human heart. The Lord gives us his Spirit within. Yet the devil makes people abuse those who have the Spirit of the Lord. But far from being astonished and afraid when this happens, we must, to the contrary, rejoice and hope. Even after the strong storm of persecution, we live in the calm hope of the Lord. In all times, we hold firmly to the gospel preached by Jesus Christ and by his disciples. They preached about the purity of the Spirit of the Lord within us and warned not to go to another. *If we preach another, that one be cursed!* The gospel teaches us that we can speak through power of the Spirit. If we in faith repudiate error and abuse, we have increased within us Jesus Christ's truth and the interior spirit.

> Am I now seeking human approval, or God's approval? Or am I trying to please people? If I were still pleasing people, I would not be a servant of Christ. (Gal 1:10)

Anyone who examines the words of Paul will see that *he is the servant of Jesus Christ.* Alas, the way he lives is very rare! Where do we find a person who does not want to please other humans and who does not instead search to find self-glory? Where do we find a person indifferent to hatred and contempt as well as love and approval? Where do we find a person who is dead to all creatures and does not skillfully aim to get their esteem? Where do we find a person who keeps God in view in all things? Yet Paul assures us that the moment we *will to please people* is the same moment we stop being *the servant of Jesus Christ.*

> For I want you to know, brothers and sisters, that the gospel that was proclaimed by me is not of human origin; 12 for I did not receive it from a human source, nor was I taught it, but I received it through a revelation of Jesus Christ. (Gal 1:11–12)

Paul describes his own life and says without hesitation that God in his mercy gave him the revelation of Jesus Christ. Paul shows us in this passage how we are to live the Christian faith. At all times we are to keep our sight on the pure glory of God in all situations. God inspires us to witness to him. We are never to keep secret what the Lord has done for us. When God acts, we witness about this to others and tell them about the Lord's mercy to us. Also, at all times, we reverently worship the Spirit of God and watch for the movements and actions of the Spirit.

We also see in this passage that Paul testifies to the good and holy *revelations* of Christ given to us. Because of the persecutions against Christians, there are people who condemn Christ's revelations saying that they are false. Corrupt ideas like this are never to be believed because they are deceptions planned by evil.

> You have heard, no doubt, of my earlier life in Judaism. I was violently persecuting the church of God and was trying to destroy it. 14 I advanced in Judaism beyond many among my people of the same age, for I was far more zealous for the traditions of my ancestors. 15 But when God, who had set me apart before I was born and called me through his grace, was pleased 16 to reveal his Son to me, so that I might proclaim him among the Gentiles, I did not confer with any human being, 17 nor did I go up to Jerusalem to those who were already apostles before me, but I went away at once into Arabia, and afterwards I returned to Damascus. (Gal 1:13–17)

Here Paul talks more about his life and freely witnesses to the grace that God gave him. Even while he describes his tradition and life, he confesses openly to his sins and faults. He does this because simple truth never hides anything. We need to speak truth because we glorify God with words of truth. We also strengthen others when we speak words of truth.

Paul describes his call from Jesus Christ and in this, we see both the goodness and strength of God. Paul openly states that he formerly opposed God's grace and violently persecuted the early church. Yet through the grace of God, Paul became the most glorious of the apostles. We see Paul's faithfulness in his response to God's call and grace by following Jesus Christ *without consulting with flesh and blood.*

We know that not everybody answers the call of Jesus Christ. In fact, some people called evade this call, and do not live for Jesus Christ. They do this because they think that their temporal interest, attachment to flesh and blood, or social situation is more important than God. Instead of doing this, they should have a trusting faith to follow the grace of God, like Paul did.

> Then after fourteen years I went up again to Jerusalem with Barnabas, taking Titus along with me. 2 I went up in response to a revelation. Then I laid before them (though only in a private meeting with the acknowledged leaders) the gospel that I proclaim among the Gentiles, in order to make sure that I was not running, or had not run, in vain. (Gal 2:1–2)

We see again in this passage how Paul was following the Spirit of the Lord and *revelation*. Therefore, he must conduct himself with faithfulness by following where the Lord shows him to go. He must not deceive others about this, but be honest and witness to others about this. When Paul speaks the truth, he is obedient to God. This applies to all faithful people.

Some wonder about revelation and how we know them to be true. In this situation we look to the witness of Scripture. If a revelation goes against Scripture, than it is to be suspected. Yet in those circumstances, we must act humanely and show others the true witness of the Lord expressed in Scripture.

No one was better led by the Spirit of the Lord than Paul. No one was more faithful to following God's movements and His grace. However, Paul does not consult other apostles because he has inside himself the light of the Spirit. Truly, he vigorously follows what is the will of God. Finally, he powerfully succeeds for the good of the church.

> But because of false believers secretly brought in, who slipped in to spy on the freedom we have in Christ Jesus, so that they might enslave us—5 we did not submit to them even for a moment, so that the truth of the gospel might always remain with you. (Gal 2:4–5)

It is amazing to see how God uses Paul who had been the greatest zealot of the law. He had forcefully and violently demanded the exact observance of the law. Now after his conversion, Paul becomes the most powerful defender of the freedom of Jesus Christ. He now ardently lives the simplicity and freedom of the Gospel. He refused to change his conduct, even if others wanted or even demanded him to change.

Paul openly admits that the church included false brothers who had come to spy on them so that they would find a way to condemn him and other believers. Yet Paul continued to witness to Jesus Christ. O the heart of a true apostle! Where does one find a person that, far from seeking to please people, actually through faith confronts them? Paul trusted the Lord, even when persecutors surrounded him.

But we wonder, how do we live our faith and help our neighbor? Paul shows us how to do this. He first established the truth of the Gospel and then he reached out to his neighbor. He lived the Gospel and made that most important. Yet in things unimportant, he cooperated and deferred to others. An example of this is when he writes, "Therefore, if food is a cause of their falling, I will never eat meat, so that I may not cause one of them to fall" (1 Cor 8:13). There is a great difference between living for propriety and self-advantage or living for the glory of God and the good of human beings. We see how Paul decided about his life and that helps us decide about ours. When he thought the issue was unimportant, he sacrifices everything for the good of his brothers. Yet Paul springs into action when he thinks the issue harms the glory of God, the foundation of the Gospel, and the community of faithful believers. O God! At that time he will not defer or change for anyone.

> But when Cephas came to Antioch, I opposed him to his face, because he stood self-condemned; 12 for until certain people came from James, he used to eat with the Gentiles. But after they came, he drew back and kept himself separate for fear of the circumcision faction. 13 And the other Jews joined him in this hypocrisy. 14 But when I saw that they were not acting consistently with the truth of the gospel, I said to Cephas before them all, "If you, though a Jew, live like a Gentile and not like a Jew, how can you compel the Gentiles to live like Jews?" (Gal 2:11–14)

In this passage, Paul defends the truth of the Gospel by confronting Peter's treatment of the Gentiles. Righteousness, which is following the will of God, is absolutely necessary. To have righteousness, we must never hide the truth. Peter, the chief among the apostles, along with the other apostles, believed their actions were charitable, yet were hiding from others that they did not follow the law anymore; their injustice would harm the Gentiles. Paul, however, could not bear that by doing this, they betrayed the truth. Paul believed that truth must go together with charity, like sisters go together. The Gospel teaches us that when we live in truth and charity, we seek justice.

The Gospel lives in our hearts and gives us righteousness. Without the Gospel within, we can never advance. When the Gospel shows us the will of God, we are blessed by faith, hope, and love. We live with the gift of these virtues and find spiritual blessing.

> For through the law, I died to the law, that I might live to God. I have been crucified with Christ. (Gal 2:19)

Paul had the revelation that the law will not carry us into faith. Because of this, he writes, "I died to the law." He writes here with great clarity saying he was dead and became a slave to the law. Because of this, he was subject to the violence of the law.

Paul realized that God wants our freedom. We are to enter into a state of perfect freedom without trouble or pain. Jesus Christ says, "Take my yoke upon you, and learn from me; for I am gentle and humble in heart; and you will find rest for your souls. For my yoke is easy, and my burden light" (Matt 11:30).

To show the relationship between the law and the Gospel freedom, Paul shows how the relationship between the law and the Gospel can be seen in his life. He says in effect, "I was a Pharisee that followed the law with the most care. I was a Grand Zealot for this law. We tried to find deliverance from sin by following the law exactly and hoped that the law would become natural."

An example of this is found in a person who studies science a long time, possesses it perfectly, and knows it naturally because of previous long hours of work. They do not study to find condemnation but want the freedom of understanding science. But how did they find this freedom? They studied and because of this, they found freedom to understand science.

Another example comes from the study of grammar. The study of grammar is useless if we cannot speak and write well. Grammar helps end ignorance and becomes a state that instructs the others. This becomes then a natural state that is acquired first by long hours of work.

But even after long hours of work and study, the law does not deliver from sins and does not give freedom. Instead, the person finds condemnation.

Jesus Christ fulfilled the law by living it perfectly. He alone lived the law naturally. When we look at him, we see the perfection of the law in a life. He did this so we may receive the promised Spirit and become his adopted children.

Paul says that he rests on this belief, "I died to the law," not violently by the law, though at times the law allowed killing. Instead, Paul died because of his sin and separation from God. I am dead constrained by the law, though I expected deliverance by following this. Paul writes, "If anyone has reason to be confident in the flesh, I have more: circumcised on the eighth day, a member of the people of Israel, of the tribe of Benjamin, a Hebrew born of Hebrews; as to the law, a Pharisee; as to zeal, a persecutor of the church; as to righteousness under the law blameless" (Phil 3:5).

Paul's revelation showed him all life comes from God. *I live with God only* that I may live by the Spirit. Through the freedom of Jesus Christ, I do not arrive at a place of self-indulgence and sensuality. Instead, with pain, suffering and work, "I am crucified with Christ Jesus."

> And it is no longer I who live, but it is Christ who lives in me. And the life I now live in the flesh I live by faith in the Son of God, who loved me and gave himself for me. (Gal 2:20)

What joy we have in this Word! Jesus Christ frees me from the law that made me dead. I live no longer by myself in the law in sensuality, corruption, and propriety. I am dead to the law. I am also dead to the law that defends me following my own inclinations. I do not live the life of propriety that was esteemed by Adam.

Now I live by faith in the Son of God. Jesus Christ lives and works in me. Jesus Christ leads and governs me. His life is my life. His Spirit communicates with me. He fills my soul with His Spirit and life. Therefore I see nothing within or without except Jesus Christ who lives within me.

This makes me dead to the law because inside I have freedom in the Spirit of Jesus Christ. Thus, I am annihilated to all things criminal and proprietary, so that I may find Jesus Christ within me. He takes away my proud exterior of conformity so *it is not anymore me that lives, but Jesus Christ living within me.* However if I *live in the flesh,* if I live again in this world with a worldly spirit that separates me from goodness, then I will live in subjection again.

Now I want to live in faith, surrender, and obedience to the Son of God. I love Him so much. I want to yield to His good will in all things to sanctify me and help me grow.

> I do not nullify the grace of God; for if justification comes through the law, then Christ died for nothing. (Gal 2:21)

If all our growth and sanctification depended on the law, then why do we have a Savior? Paul understands that we need a Savior and tells us of the grace merited by Jesus Christ; also, Paul says, "In him we have

8

redemption through his blood, the forgiveness of our trespasses, according to the riches of his grace that he lavished on us" (Ephesians 1:7–8). This abundant redemption is made through Jesus Christ's death. This rigorous death was essential for the salvation of human beings. The actions of Jesus were sufficient for the redemption of a million worlds, as he willed salvation for our abundant redemption. By his death he destroyed in all of us the life of Adam. Following the law brings us death. If we hope to acquire this perfection through the law, we make *the death of Jesus Christ in vain*, since he died so that we may die to this law. If we give and attribute all to the law, we receive nothing from His grace of justification. We must die to the law and live to Jesus Christ.

> You foolish Galatians! Who has bewitched you? It was before your eyes that Jesus Christ was publicly exhibited as crucified! (Gal 3:1)

Nothing is as hard as the sight of these people that before had received pure grace now leave this way and then return to their former madness. These are people that have known the favorable effects of grace and tasted the sweet prayer and presence of God; they have been instructed in God's ways and had *Jesus Christ depicted before their eyes*. That is to say, the preachers of the Gospel (with whom Jesus Christ is well pleased) depicted the crucifixion for them. After this, they have had *Jesus Christ crucified* and manifested within them. Even after all these things, they leave Jesus Christ, often because of false reports, under the pretext of a more accurate gospel. O, this is very hard to bear from people who had been educated in the truth!

> The only thing I want to learn from our is this: Did you receive the Spirit by doing the works of the law or by believing what you heard? (Gal 3:2)

This question goes to all people who have received the anointing of the Holy Spirit and grace within the interior. Is it by *doing the law that you have received the Spirit* of love, peace and charity? No, assuredly. The *word that you have heard* the Lord speak inside of you gives his Spirit and the anointing of His grace.

> Are you so foolish? Having started with the Spirit, are you now ending with the flesh? (Gal 3:3)

After having suffered to be with God, we make our sufferings useless, since we return to our first madness. There are persons who return to sin after having left them; for others, after having been advanced in the way of the Spirit, they quit to follow nature; for others, after having left propriety for the way of surrender to Jesus Christ, leave Jesus Christ and return to the way of propriety. Now these people, having suffered much travail, have made their pains and sufferings vain and useless.

> Just as Abraham "believed God, and it was reckoned to him as righteousness," 7 so, you see, those who believe are the descendants of Abraham. (Gal 3:6–7)

The principal character of Abraham was his faith and his abandon to the rule of God. Abraham believed and trusted in God's promises; he respected God's strong rule and followed Him, even when the way seemed to destroy the promises. That is what makes Abraham's perfect state and is what distinguishes his character from the rest of humanity. Like Abraham, the true characteristics of interior souls are faith and abandon. Faith is their foundation and prayers make their interior. Their exterior conduct is to abandon to God and to follow his step-by-step providence. They receive the will of God moment to moment, and trust God in all situations, both the bad and the good. Abraham's children are those with interior grace. These children have faith and abandon to the rule of God and receive this rule through true contemplation. This character of the interior soul distinguishes these people from others. These interior people are the true children of Abraham.

> And the Scriptures, foreseeing that God would justify the Gentiles by faith, declared the gospel beforehand to Abraham, saying, "All the Gentiles shall be blessed in you." 9 For this reason, those who believe are blessed with Abraham who believed. (Gal 3:8–9)

Scriptures prophesied the true justification of faith. God says that all the nations will be blessed by Abraham. God gave Abraham faith and abandon, and, through Abraham, his strong blessing flows out to all the nations. We may be good and virtuous without entering into the state of faith, leading a settled and good life. But for perfect justification, we must enter faith. Therefore, we receive the blessing along with Abraham, the gift of faith.

> For all who rely on the works of the law are under a curse; for it is written, "Cursed is everyone who does not observe and obey all the things written in the book of the law." 11 Now it is evident that no one is justified before God by the law; for "The one who is righteous will live by faith." (Gal 3:10–11)

Those who trust the works of the law are mistaken and bring on themselves the curse that makes them guilty. The law has power only because of its ability to condemn and kill. Because the law is ultimately based in violence, it cannot be depended upon to save and deliver. We understand that the law does not communicate grace, because the threat and use of violence must accomplish the law. Hence, the believer cannot have confidence in the works of the law. Instead, we put all our trust in the grace of God merited by Jesus Christ, who accomplished the law perfectly. He fulfilled the law by grace as he lived the will of his Father. Jesus Christ trusted his Father.

The consequence of this belief is clear. *The just live by faith*; therefore to be justified, live by faith. To be justified, let us live faith. When we live this faith, we will be just since the just live by faith. This argument suffers no contradictions.

> But the law does not rest on faith; on the contrary, "Whoever does the works of the law will live by them."13 Christ redeemed us from the curse of the law by becoming a curse for us—for it is written, "Cursed is everyone who hangs on a tree." (Gal 3:12–13)

The law in itself does not establish trust in faith. It stops before faith. The law does not have the Spirit and is ignorant of the way of faith.

Jesus Christ delivers us from the heavy burden of the law with its servitude and curse. Instead, Jesus Christ works in our hearts so that we abandon ourselves to him and walk in faith. Paul writes that Jesus Christ delivers us from the observation of the law since it is contrary to the words of Jesus Christ. "Do not think that I have come to abolish the law or the prophets; I have come not to abolish but to fulfill" (Matt 5:17). Therefore by his death, Jesus Christ accomplishes the fulfillment of the law. He came to *deliver us from the curse of the law*, that is to say, the heavy slavery of the law. The violence of the law is a heavy yoke upon our hearts. Instead, the yoke of Jesus Christ is gentle and humble in heart. Jesus says, "For my yoke is easy and my burden light" (Luke 11:30).

But how does Jesus Christ deliver us from this harsh servitude? It is by *making himself cursed for us*, he places himself under all the rigors of the law with full responsibility for this heavy burden. By doing so, he delivers us from the severity of the law and fulfills the justice of His Father. He places in us perfect grace and makes this easy by the power and efficacy of his love. We must not look upon his love as a law, but as a pleasure greater than the world, that carries us with sweetness and with nothing contrary to

God's good will. We obey God and he delivers us from slavery to the law. For us, we remain in God's sweetness and graciousness.

Why do people stay with the violence and difficulty of the law? They do not walk in the Spirit but they trust only in the law. They accomplish things only with strange violence. This new life of faith seems impossible to them, and instead of this, they want the pleasure and ease of the world. Because they do not want this faith, they enter into death.

> In order that in Christ Jesus the blessing of Abraham might come to the Gentiles, so that we might receive the promise of the Spirit through faith. (Gal 3:14)

The blessing of Abraham is the Spirit of the Lord that brings faith and abandon. This communicates to us the promises of Jesus Christ. But do all Christians receive the Spirit? No, because not all Christians trust Jesus Christ. Instead, they trust their own actions and propriety. They do not trust God.

> Brothers and sisters, I give an example from daily life: once a person's will has been ratified, no one adds to it or annuls it. 16 Now the promises were made to Abraham and to him offspring; it does not say, "And to your offsprings," as of many; but it says, "And to your offspring," that is, to one person, who is Christ. 17 My point is this: the law, which came four hundred thirty years later, does not annul a covenant previously ratified by God, so as to nullify the promise. (Gal 3:15–17)

God gave his promise as a gift so we could have the freedom of his children. This promise was made before the law was given. The law does not mean the end of God's promises. Faith tells us that the promises are ours. Therefore, by faith and not by the law is Jesus Christ received in the heart. The law does not abolish the promise but is given as a favor of the promise.

God gave the law as a pledge of the fulfillment of the promise. The law serves as a forerunner of Jesus Christ. Once Jesus Christ came, the law was finished because Jesus Christ was the end and consummation of the law. Jesus Christ confirms the strength of the law because the law leads us to Jesus Christ. But once we have arrived in Jesus Christ, the way of the law ceases, because we have entered into Jesus Christ and faith. The law is finished as a way but is not destroyed and abolished. To the contrary, the law helps us see

Jesus Christ and his perfection. The law is reunited in the end and perfectly consummated where all becomes one in Jesus Christ.

> For if the inheritance comes from the law, it no longer comes from the promise; but God granted it to Abraham through the promise. 19 Why, then, the law? It was added because of transgressions, until the offspring would come to whom the promise had been made; and it was ordained through angels by a mediator. (Gal 3:18–19)

Our inheritance comes from God and our inheritance is God. God promised an inheritance to Abraham and the inheritance is Jesus Christ. This promised faith gives us the Jesus Christ.

We see that the gift of Jesus Christ did not come to us through the law. If Jesus Christ were given to us through the law, he would have been the reward and recompense of the law. God made the promise before the law; the promise is not the reward of the law.

But why, says Paul to himself as an objection, *is the law given to us*, if the law does not give Jesus Christ? The law, he responds, has been given *to stop sin*; the law is given as a way to view sin and a way to lead us to Jesus Christ, since the law introduces the person to the faith and this communicates Jesus Christ. Therefore the law must be given first and the person was initially subject to the law, so that sin was clearly seen. The law shows sin but cannot completely destroy it. The law was prepared and given to humanity by angels. These are not communications made by Jesus Christ but by the intermediaries of ministering angels.

Yet this subjection to the law was absolutely necessary. This is the narrow door that holds the person still in order to prevent sin while God purifies the soul. The reason for this is that the people use their choices for sin so God wants to abolish sin so the person will return to God. The law provides a necessary purification through the mediation of angels.

But this state of servitude that appears perfect will never communicate Jesus Christ himself who is *the Son of the promise*. Only Jesus Christ gives us himself.

This law is the way of introduction, since it leads the soul to the pure faith, where it may never enter unless purified by the way of the law. This law helps us grow by keeping us captive and still. This law holds the person in an interior state that does not waste its energies externally. The external law regulates everything and takes away false pleasures. Later faith takes the place of the law. This faith puts the person in the freedom of Jesus Christ therefore *you have died to the law through the body of Christ* (Rom 7:6). Now the person is freed to make good choices without malice or sin.

The effect of Jesus Christ's redemption is that he ransoms us not only from the wrath of God, but also from the wickedness and iniquity communicated to us through malice and sin.

But it must be noted that to arrive, we must pass through the law. Whoever believes that he or she will arrive in Jesus without passing through the law is wrong. The law provides a needed purification. It is an illusion in the spiritual life that people believe that they arrive in Jesus Christ without having passed through the law with its purification. We are wrong to think that we can arrive in freedom without the law. This is not liberty but libertinism. Some people wander off from the law. Hence, they lose true devotion and truth itself.

> Now a mediator involves more than one party; but God is one. (Gal 3:20)

The promise given to Abraham was made without a mediator. Jesus Christ is united to us in faith also without a mediator. So the law is not a mediator. *God alone* gives us the power to receive the promise. Faith leads us to this union. Jesus Christ is hidden in the Father and we are hidden in them.

> Is the law then opposed to the promises of God? Certainly not! For if a law had been given that could make alive, then righteousness would indeed come through the law. 22 But the Scripture has imprisoned all things under the power of sin, so that what was promised through faith in Jesus Christ might be given to those who believe. (Gal 3:21–22)

The law is not opposed to the promise; to the contrary, because the law, as it was written, was given as a favor to the promise. The promise was not made for the law, but the law for the promise. Therefore the law is not opposed to the promise, as we have seen in understanding the previous Scriptures.

So if the law communicates life, justice would come through the law, but justice is not able to come through a principle. The law does not have life in itself but only brings death. It is Jesus Christ that has life in himself and he gave himself to communicate life to others. The law is not contrary to justice but it does not have the power to communicate justice. To the contrary, it prepares people to receive justice that must be communicated by faith in Jesus Christ.

That is to say, Scripture shows that the law has no power over sin. The law does not communicate life but shows sin. Jesus Christ destroys the substance of sin that is the source of death, as he communicates life.

Therefore it is through faith in Jesus Christ that the promise is given. This promise is Jesus Christ himself, who remakes the believer with him in the first vitality and in its original being before the fall that began human sin.

> Now before faith came, we were imprisoned and guarded under the law until faith would be revealed. Therefore the law was our disciplinarian until Christ came, so that we might be justified by faith. (Gal 3:23–24)

My Lord, these passages are so clear that explain your goodness in this chapter! Paul says that before pure faith was communicated in Jesus Christ, we were held in custody under law. This law guarded and held us. We were captive under the law so we did not sin. And in this captivity, we were prepared little by little for faith. Yet while in captivity, we were uncertain if there was really something better for us. The heart hopes for something, but does not yet possess it. This law desires faith that will banish sins and purify the inclinations from the habit of sin, but it cannot fulfill this desire. The law serves as a tutor to teach the soul about the beginning of the spiritual life. This tutor leads the soul to Jesus Christ. The person is not withdrawn from sin by law for the person is only justified by faith.

> But now that faith has come, we are no longer subject to a disciplinarian, 26 for in Christ Jesus you are all children of God through faith. (Gal 3: 25–26)

But now that faith has come, we are no longer under a disciplinarian. We are delivered from our captivity under the law. It is clear that the law cannot destroy our sins and so the law was finished. Jesus Christ can destroy sins, and not only our sins, but even the roots of sin. Jesus Christ gives his life and banishes the cause of death. His resurrection destroyed death itself. Paul expresses this powerful belief in all of his writings.

Therefore, we are not under subjection to the law since faith has been given to us. We have Jesus Christ. Previously we practiced the law, like a child previously has learned lessons.

To be delivered from the law does not mean that we live opposed to the law. To the contrary, we see the perfection of the law. He gives us faith and we are freed from death. He communicates justice and we are delivered from all injustice. This good state of faith has perfection and eternity, and takes away original sin; nothing remains to make us captive. We see in Jesus Christ the living law. Jesus Christ contains all the law and lived the law naturally. Because of this, through His grace, we too are freed from slavery and placed in this perfect freedom.

But how do we find this freedom? Leaving forever the state of servitude and slavery, we become God's sons and daughters and this spirit of being a child gives us freedom. Paul explains elsewhere, "For all who are led by the Spirit of God are children of God. For you did not receive a spirit of slavery to fall back into fear, but you have received a spirit of adoption. When we cry 'Abba! Father!' it is the very Spirit bearing witness with our spirit that we are children of God" (Rom 8:14–15). According to this word, we become children and enter into the freedom of a child, and leave forever the place of slavery.

O wonderful truth! How is it that all Christians do not comprehend this point? All Christians do not feel and taste this truth. They never give themselves to Jesus Christ so they will become free. They remain slaves to the demons and the law so they remain without freedom and deceived by sin. They will not give and abandon themselves to the Spirit. They do not have a present faith but they still guide themselves by the law. They wish to remain in this way and never find the way of faith.

O Truth that is pure and essential to the Christian faith! You are the heart of religion! Almost all Christians are ignorant of this. They do not want the body of faith and they do not live by the Spirit.

> As many of you as were baptized into Christ have clothed yourselves with Christ. 28 There is no longer Jew or Greek, there is no longer slave or free, there is no longer male and female; for all of you are one in Christ Jesus. (Gal 3:27–28)

If we remember Jesus Christ's baptism in John and Matthew, we see clearly the similarity between the Gospels and Paul's letters. This will show what we say here. John's baptism was based on the law and penitence that leads us to Jesus Christ. John said, "I baptize you with water for repentance" (Matt 3:11). Also Jesus Christ said to John, "Let it be so now; for it is proper for us in this way to fulfill all righteousness" (Matt 3:15). The baptism of John was the law's purification. This is why it does not communicate life and justice. John the Baptist prepared hearts to receive Jesus. However, the baptism of Jesus Christ communicates to us the Spirit of Jesus Christ, which is the Spirit of life. Jesus Christ fulfilled the law. After Jesus' baptism, "the heavens were opened to him, and he saw the Spirit of God descending like a dove, and alighting on him" (Matt 3:16). This was why after John baptized Jesus Christ, the Spirit descended on Christ like a dove to show us that his baptism gives us Spirit and life. Jesus communicates to us his Spirit and justice. It also gives us the exterior of Jesus Christ that we put on as clothing.

Jesus Christ gives us both his interior and his exterior. He communicates his interior to us with his Spirit. If we are baptized in Jesus Christ, we receive the Spirit of Jesus Christ and our exterior life is conformed to his. If our lives do not conform to his, we do not share our interior with him. We can live a virtuous life but it is not properly a life of grace if Jesus Christ does not animate us.

After the person is baptized, little by little the person becomes united to God. There is no distinction between the Jews and Gentiles, which means, there is no difference between those who have grace and those who are lost but will be found. There is no difference between the strong and the weak. All is in God and God has all power.

> And if you belong to Christ, then you are Abraham's offspring, heirs according to the promise. (Gal 3:29)

Paul concludes by saying that the promise given to Abraham tells us we inherit the faith. We *enter into Jesus Christ by faith*. Those who are in Jesus Christ are heirs of Abraham, according to the promise given to him.

> My point is this: heirs, as long as they are minors, are no better than slaves though they are the owners of all property, 2 but they remain under guardians and trustees until the date set by the father. 3 So with us; while we were minors, we were enslaved to the elemental spirits of the world. (Gal 4:1–3)

All are begotten in Jesus Christ by baptism. They begin in spiritual infancy and need to receive the quality of a son or daughter. If during the spiritual childhood the quality of a son or daughter is not received, then they will always remain in servitude and will never enter into freedom.

Some souls God raises by his absolute power without passing through this way.

> But when the fullness of time had come, God sent his son, born of a woman, born under the law, 5 in order to redeem those who

were under the law, so that we might receive adoption as children. (Gal 4:4–5)

But how did he come? In the fullness of time, the Word incarnate was formed in Mary. After the time of slavery, Jesus Christ was formed in a woman, in human weakness and powerlessness, so that he could come to us. God used a human woman to form Jesus Christ. Like Mary, we receive the Word of Jesus Christ within our hearts.

How is the Word produced in hearts? When believers are worn out with their limited understanding, then God's fullness moves into their empty lives. These new graces are eminent and fill the life. The plenitude of graces in a life forms Jesus Christ within.

As we have seen, the fullness of grace in our life is very wonderful. We are astonished at the fullness of grace poured upon us, as it is says in the Scriptures. When we receive the fullness of grace God pours upon us, we know the wonderful consummation of life. This consummation of pure fulfillment forms Jesus Christ within us.

Jesus Christ wanted to submit to the law so that he could redeem the law. We know Christ's redemption in the joy of the promise and our divine adoption as children. No one will reach the grace of adoption without passing through the servitude of the law, although no one should remain subject to the law.

Through Abraham we understand that there are two types of children. One is the child of servitude to the law. The child of servitude is not the child of promise. Abraham wanted to adopt the servant but what did the Lord answer? "But the word of the Lord came to him: 'This man shall not be your heir; no one but your very own issue shall be your heir'" (Gen 15:4). The child of servitude does not inherit, but the inheritance is given to the child of promise. The children of servitude have nothing spiritual and have only the end of a sword. All these people remain in their servitude and they have nothing but combat. All their lives pass in fighting and violence. They do not have the great virtues of faith, hope and love, and they do not have the effect of the promise, that is the formation of Jesus Christ within and the freedom of adopted children.

Scriptures showing this are drawn from three locations: Genesis 15:2–4, 17:20–21, and 27:40. Children of servitude are Eliezer, Ishmael, and Esau. Though these look like three different examples, actually they are one united response opposed to the children of freedom. That is all we need to say.

The children of freedom are the second type. They leave behind servitude to the law for the joy of freedom. These adopted children do not fight pointlessly. They have joy in the freedom as sons and daughters. Jesus Christ is formed within them and he fights for them. Jesus Christ redeems them from slavery that is the sign of the servitude of the law. Instead, Jesus Christ places them in freedom.

> And because you are children, God has sent the Spirit of his Son into our hearts, crying, "Abba! Father!" 7 So you are no longer a slave but a child, and if a child then also an heir, through God. (Gal 4:6–7)

If we have believed in the Son of God without doubting, we are called into the freedom of being his children. We are attached to him through this adoption. But how do we recognize if we are children of God? Paul says that *if you are a child of God, God has placed in your hearts the Spirit of his Son*. Therefore, no external sign tells us of our adoption, but we know this through the interior life of the Spirit of Jesus Christ. So we leave behind servitude and become a child when we live in the Spirit of Jesus Christ. We must be led and governed by the Spirit of Jesus Christ. This Spirit prays within our souls.

If therefore we are the children of God who the Spirit prays within with power, we let the Spirit guide us. It is clear that in the Spirit of surrender to God, we pray freely. We do not follow the spirit of propriety but the movement of the Spirit of God. I say that it is certain that the prayer of abandonment, faith, and docility, makes the difference between the children and the servants. God sends his Spirit who prays and sighs for us as children, yet does not do this on his servants. *If we are children, then we are heirs of Jesus Christ*; consequently we are those to whom Jesus Christ gives his inheritance. My God! If we understand well the sense of these words, then we will never leave you! The people that believe this, though disparaged and treated as the scum of the world, are God's children.

> You know it was because of a physical infirmity that I first announced the gospel to you; 14 though my condition put you to the test, you did not scorn or despise me, but welcomed me as an angel of God, as Christ Jesus. (Gal 4:13–14)

Temptations come even in the apostolic state. Yet here Paul remembers their shared beginning with humility and talks openly about his illness. Through his humility he makes the strongest case against their propriety and overbearing pride. The strongest sign of abandonment to God is this simplicity and candor in opening up about misery. A humble person has no difficulty talking about weakness, but a proud and proprietary person does not talk openly about pain. A person with spiritual understanding is not surprised and scandalized by weakness; to the contrary, they understand this as a good sign. Paul says to the Galatians that *they welcomed him as an angel and like Jesus Christ himself* in the beginning when he was devastated with heavy burdens of the flesh. Now he asks, in the new life in which I have been placed, why do you not receive me more eagerly now?

> What has become of the goodwill you felt? For I testify that, had it been possible, you would have torn out your eyes and given them to me. (Gal 4:15)

When we bring everything simply to God, what sweetness we taste, what pleasure we have in God! What joy we have in our heart and what gratitude to our ministers for telling us this! But if people turn away from the gospel, they turn away from truth and reject their pastors. Then sadly our best friend can become our enemy simply by telling us the truth.

> My little children, for whom I am again in the pain of childbirth until Christ is formed in you. (Gal 4:19)

Paul speaks with the feelings of a true apostle. There are two moments of grace in conversion. The first is when the person becomes converted when, tired of sin, the person is born into the life of grace. The second is when Jesus Christ is formed within. The second happens when, tired of being led by propriety, the person enters into Jesus Christ. This is when we leave the exterior world to enter into the interior. We quit our corrupted and ruined life of propriety to come alive again in the new life of Jesus Christ. This is the time when Jesus Christ is formed in us.

> I wish I were present with you now and could change my tone, for I am perplexed about you. (Gal 4:20)

When an apostle knows that believers hear the pure voice of the Spirit, then he hopes for their spiritual advancement. Yet now, far from benefitting from Paul's words as they did in the beginning, these people abuse him and regret having spoken with him openly. Paul wishes to speak with them in their former closeness. With sadness he sees that pearls have been tossed before swine. Yet God has all the glory.

Paul is careful to preach the truth about the interior: how it is present and that this truth is strongly combatted by external and literal forces. Yet Scripture shows that God fights for the truth of the interior. O God! You make known your truth in the interior like you manifest it in the exterior! O God! Have pity on your church! Lord, as in Revelation, the pregnant woman who is full of your Spirit, wants to give birth to the child for all of your children. The dragon is before the woman, making his efforts to take away the fruit. But you, Lord, guard the fruit in your being and the dragon is sent down to the earth. As the Psalmist says, "When you send forth your spirit, they are created; and you renew the face of the ground" Psalm 104:30. My God! Have pity on your children. They are more attacked than ever before. Preserve, Lord, your Spirit in all your people. You can, and you must, O Divine Savior, who is the church's Spouse. I hear your secret and profound voice saying to me: "I will establish," says the Spirit, "by the same things that seem designed to destroy it, as I first established my Church in what seemed to destroy it at its birth." To this, Lord Jesus, your servant responds, "Amen! Amen, Lord Jesus! Come, O desire of the nations! Come! The Prophets and Patriarchs long for you! Come!" "I will come. Amen."

> For it is written that Abraham had two sons, one by a slave woman and the other by a free woman. 23 One, the child of the slave, was born according to the flesh; the other, the child of the free woman, was born through the promise. (Gal 4:22–23)

Human beings are composed of nature and grace. The child of God was born in grace and justice. But at the same time was born a child of concupiscence from the flesh because of sin. And this son of the slave was a sinner and criminal, born only from the flesh. But the son of freedom, that is grace, was born only from the promise. When we are born, we are all children of the slave, but at our baptism we become children of the promise by the grace of Jesus Christ. However, nature grows along with grace, and servitude accompanies freedom.

> But just as at that time the child who was born according to the flesh persecuted the child who was born according to the Spirit, so it is now also. (Gal 4:29)

The children of the flesh, which are nature and slavery, fight incessantly against the children of the Spirit and persecute those with the Spirit without giving them a rest. These children of the flesh revolt continually because of sin.

But what does the Scripture say? "Drive out the slave and her child; for the child of the slave will not share the inheritance with the child of the freewoman." 31 So then, friends, we are children, not of the slave but of the free woman. 5:1 For freedom Christ has set us free. (Gal 4:30—5:1)

What are we to do? We must leave everything that has to do with nature, because it has no part in God or in grace. All the works of nature, even if they appear sublime, have no part in the operations of God and grace. Therefore, it is necessary to find and destroy the works of nature, to die to the natural, because to live is to have grace. Through Jesus Christ we are freed from slavery, and it is our advantage to be guided by Jesus Christ. We abandon ourselves to him without reservation, because we are in him. We are not, writes Paul, children of the slave, but we are free, and it is Jesus Christ who gives us freedom.

> For through the Spirit, by faith, we eagerly wait for the hope of righteousness. 6 For in Christ Jesus neither circumcision nor uncircumcision counts for anything; the only thing that counts is faith working through love. (Gal 5:5–6)

Exterior people believe themselves to be just and feel that their works justify themselves. Yet interior people do not see justice in themselves because they know that Jesus Christ communicates his justice to their interior. Because of this, these interior persons realize that they contribute nothing to this justice. They see that all is in God and of God. They are convinced that circumcision or uncircumcision only makes conflict. Only faith is essential. This faith lives inside and works both in the interior and exterior in love and perfect charity.

> For you were called to freedom, brothers and sisters; only do not use your freedom as an opportunity for self-indulgence, but through love become slaves to one another. (Gal 5:13)

This belief has the greatest consequence. God calls us to be interior and have freedom. The interior spirit is peace, joy, and freedom. But it is a magnificent consequence of this to remain in the freedom of the Spirit and not to enter into the freedom of the flesh, as many people do. They leave the Spirit behind and live in the ways of the flesh. They become convinced that their freedom consists in sensual and carnal acts.

Instead, freedom happens when we abandon ourselves to the will of God. The person does not retain anything for propriety, even as minor as propriety might appear. Propriety is not for us because we are introduced to freedom. God gives us a different place, as it is written: "So if the Son makes you free, you will be free indeed" (John 8:36). This freedom will be the freedom of the Son, in the operations of the Son, and not a carnal freedom, in the operations of the flesh. Also, Paul has spoken of this freedom, saying that the children of the servant had to be driven out. They have the operations of nature that enter into carnal freedom but when the children of the slave are driven out, there is nothing to fear. In opposition to this, we have the freedom of the Spirit.

> Live by the Spirit, I say, and do not gratify the desires of the flesh.
> (Gal 5:16)

Whoever wants to be free and not live under subjection to the flesh must live according to the Spirit. Most people are destroyed by their unbalanced desires and carnal passions. The way out of these passions is to be interior. Paul writes that we must not fulfill the desires of the flesh. Instead, we live according to the Spirit and become interior and spiritual. If we disparage the interior, we live in carnal sin. Paul says that a carnal person lies if he says he is interior. The true interior is peace, chastity, and all the rest of the fruits of the Holy Spirit.

> For what the flesh desires is opposed to the Spirit, and what the Spirit desires is opposed to the flesh; for these are opposed to each other, to prevent you from doing what you want. 18 But if you are led by the Spirit, you are not subject to the law. (Gal 5:17–18)

When guided by the spirit of propriety, we become part of that double and strange combat of the flesh against the spirit. This combat is sometimes violent and always damaging. The Spirit has desires, and the flesh has desires. This causes a strange opposition between the Spirit and the flesh. The children of the slave must be driven out. In time they will be moved and chased away by the Spirit and when this happens, we lose the spirit of servitude and enter into freedom. Then we are not subjected to the law and this combat. The law is for the flesh and not for the Spirit. The Spirit is not the law. In the Spirit we adore and love God.

> Now the works of the flesh are obvious: fornication, impurity, licentiousness, 20 idolatry, sorcery, enmities, strife, jealousy, anger, quarrels, dissensions, factions, envy, drunkenness, carousing, and things like these. I am warning you, as I warned you before: those

who do such things will not inherit the Kingdom of God. (Gal
5:19–21)

We cannot be mistaken in a matter of this great importance. Paul gives
us the true signs that are connected with the freedom of the flesh and the
freedom of the Spirit. The freedom of the flesh produces these works of the
flesh that Paul decries; these carnal works are bad fruits and never spiritual
ones.

> By contrast, the fruit of the Spirit is love, joy, peace, patience, kind-
> ness, generosity, faithfulness, 23 gentleness, and self-control. (Gal
> 5:22)

The Spirit of Jesus Christ produces the true characteristics of interior
people. Here is true freedom. When seeing these good fruits, Paul assures
us that these come from the Holy Spirit. But if these are the true effects
found in interior people, why do some condemn them as if they were
guilty? Why then would those who have these be condemned as if they
had an evil spirit? This is a very great injustice that happens to those who
serve God. The fruits of the Spirit or the fruits of the flesh: if the fruits are
of the Spirit, he or she is spiritual. But if the fruits are of the flesh, we know
that he or she is acting on carnal feelings. How do we arrive at this? Some
condemn those who have these fruits of the Spirit and do not find good in
these fruits. Instead, they find malignity in these trees bearing fruit. But
how can they believe and judge these trees to be evil when they produce
such excellent fruits? Isn't this the lowest form of injustice? Yet that is what
we do today to interior and spiritual people.

> There is no law against such things. (Gal 5:23b)

The law is against crime and is not against just human beings. The
law condemns murder and adultery. The law does not condemn charity
and continence. The point is to be delivered from the law and not to be
subjected to the law. We are to be interior and spiritual. Because according
to Paul, the law is not against those who live in sweetness, modesty, and
charity. Those that live in this way are those who are interior. We walk according to the Spirit. Therefore, the law is not against interior people, but is
against those who are not.

> And those who belong to Christ Jesus have crucified the flesh with
> its passions and desires. 25 If we live by the Spirit, let us also be
> guided by the Spirit. (Gal 5:24–25)

We assume that we must crucify these passions by our penitence, yet this is an error. Some people say that we will never be in Jesus Christ unless we ourselves first crucify our vices, passions, flesh, concupiscence, and evil desires by strong and frequent exercises of mortification. It is false to believe that we must crucify these things. Instead, God through providence gives us situations that will crucify us.

It is necessary that John the Baptist came before and prepared hearts to receive Jesus Christ. Jesus needed Elijah to come first, as is explained in Matthew.

Now, we must remember only what Jesus Christ says to his disciples that those who are in Him and listen to the voice of the Spirit do not need penitence. Jesus Christ says that those who are with the Bridegroom in his presence do not mourn. We fast only when the Bridegroom leaves. Jesus said, "The wedding guests cannot mourn as long as the bridegroom is with them, can they? The days will come when the bridegroom is taken away from them, and then they will fast" (Matt 9:15).

The Evangelist shows that we do not fast when we have the Bridegroom. If we live the spiritual life, we must walk only in the Spirit. It is necessary that the exterior correspond to the interior.

> My friends, if anyone is detected in a transgression, you who have received the Spirit should restore such a one in a spirit of gentleness. Take care that you yourselves are not tempted. (Gal 6:1)

The spirit of gentleness is very effective to restore those who are given to another spirit. If we are truly humble and persuade those who have fallen into a fault, it is the effect of a singular grace. We have gentleness for sinners and we watch for defiance within ourselves. We make a good path for those who have fallen low. This is what Paul says: "Work out your own salvation with fear and trembling" (Phil 2:12). Because when we are trusting and abandoned to God, when we look at God, we do not see profound misery, without discovering a pure and perfect action to do. O God! When you raise us to your height, our interior is purified. When we are placed in the crucible, we see inside ourselves what previously seemed full of order. O the impurity of the creature, who can comprehend this? O the purity of God! That is eternal and inconceivable! There is nothing good and pure within us. "God puts no trust even in his holy ones, and the heavens are not clean in his sight" (Job 15:15). I say before God I have had no pure or good actions in my life that God has not made within me. O God! That which appears pure is impure before you! But the highest grace of all graces is that you know the truth in the soul and that you put within us strength in this truth.

> Bear one another's burdens, and in this way you will fulfill the law of Christ. For if those who are nothing think they are something, they deceive themselves. (Gal 6:2–3)

In true charity we carry the burdens and imperfections of others, both their natural and spiritual weakness. My God! I believe that true perfection and perfect charity occurs when we carry with equanimity, gentleness and patience the faults of others. That means when they suffer, we suffer with them.

Also, our soul advances when we truthfully see that we are nothing. O deceit and the deceitfulness of souls! Being nothing, we feel humble before God and before humanity, both in nature and in grace! We are nothing. O truth that is well designed in the state of nothingness! We must be perfectly annihilated to know and comprehend truth because we are nothing.

> All must test their own work; then that work, rather than their neighbor's work, will become a cause for pride. (Gal 6:4)

We can examine ourselves in two different ways. One is through the propriety of the creature and the other is the way of God. In propriety we examine ourselves with the light of self-love, that we may see our actions to show our goodness and hide our faults. It is somber and false that we do this; it is deception and not through light that we do this. It is like the shadowy light of a chandelier shining on us. If we refuse to see ourselves with the light of God, we are lost.

But to examine ourselves through God is like the light of his Sun. It is profound and brilliant. We find faults within. The souls that are viewed only by the chandelier's torch appear beautiful but they deceive themselves. Instead, when seen clearly in God's adorable Sun, we are horrified at ourselves. These people cry out in astonishment, All my justice is before you as nothingness or false!

O God, what a difference to see ourselves through eyes of propriety, or to see through the eyes of God! I am astonished at this. If it does not come from God, it is not to be trusted. As Isaiah writes, "There is no one who calls on your name, or attempts to take hold of you; for you have hidden your face from us, and have delivered us into the hand of our iniquity" (Isa 64:7).

Only love lives in assurance, because love consumes all that is impure within us. We are blind if we do not look at You! We are like the Cherubim who tremble before the Angels who represent all knowledge. In humility we tremble before God. When we move toward pure love, it pleases God to send us a ray of knowledge to show how we truly are, even if it fills us with horror. God acts and allows us to approach with perfect trust, even when we are fearful and terrified. We will not be judged by the esteem or contempt of creatures, but by the light of God.

> Those who are taught the word must share in all good things with their teacher. 7 Do not be deceived; God is not mocked, for you reap whatever you sow. (Gal 6: 6–7)

All the works that are made and animated in the Spirit are good and holy works. But the works conceived by corrupt principles are self-love and vainglory. There are some people who falsely say that if we are interior, we will not do good works. To the contrary, it is self-love that corrupts and stops good works. Works that have no foundation in the interior are vicious and decaying. They only try to deceive. Those who prefer themselves with their inclinations will reject the pleasure found in Jesus Christ. They then live only in the flesh and will find only corruption. Instead, those who live for Jesus Christ will receive life and immortality.

> May I never boast of anything except the cross of our Lord Jesus Christ, by which the world has been crucified to me, and I to the world. (Gal 6:14)

O happy state that a person has found God's glory in suffering, pain, ignominies, abjections, and finally in the cross and all that goes along with the cross. The world crucified Jesus Christ, as the world does his followers. What does it mean to be crucified as he was crucified in the world? It is when we do not believe in the world and that we do not want to taste its pleasure. We know that everything in the world moves in bitterness. Worldly people desire pleasures that we believers would find a torment. *The world to us is crucified.* The world hates faithful people. Jesus Christ said, "If you belonged to the world, the world would love you as its own. Because you do not belong to the world, but I have chosen you out of the world— therefore the world hates you" (John 15:19). The world hates these strong believers and their gospel foundation, so it gives them a thousand crosses. It makes a point of persecuting them. Finally, I cannot explain it better than to say that we are crucified to the world, as the world is crucified to us.

> For neither circumcision nor uncircumcision is anything; but a new creation is everything! (Gal 6:15)

The law was useful once but it is now utterly useless. There is only one thing that is absolutely necessary and that is to be a new creation. But how do we become a new creation? This is by leaving behind the old human being of Adam, the sinner. As Paul says, "So if anyone is in Christ, there is a new creation: everything old has passed away; see, everything has become new!" (2 Cor 5:17). We must be in Jesus Christ so that everything from Adam is gone. This is the necessary choice.

> As for those who will follow this rule—peace be upon them, and mercy, and upon the Israel of God. (Gal 6:16)

Peace and mercy are found perfectly by all who follow this pure rule: let go all that came from Adam, the sinner. To continue holding on to Adam and sin destroys peace and prevents the freedom of us tasting the new creation in Jesus Christ. Peace blesses those who are led by God, that is to say, to abandoned souls like Israel.

> From now on, let no one make troubles for me; for I carry the marks of Jesus branded on my body. (Gal 6:17)

Nobody, says Paul, afflicts and increases my pain, because I have already surpassed living by my natural powers. *I carry on my body the marks of Jesus Christ.* Christ's external sufferings are marked on me. I therefore carry the states of Jesus Christ. That means "always carrying in the body the death of Jesus, so that the life of Jesus may also be made visible in our bodies" (2 Cor 4:10) and carrying the crucified state of Jesus Christ. O those that carry these marks are happy! O love, it is a great good to share the sufferings of this life with you, so that we may reign with you!

Guyon's *Commentary on Paul's Letter to the Ephesians with Explanations and Reflections on the Interior Life*

> Paul, an apostle of Christ Jesus by the will of God. To the saints who are also faithful in Christ Jesus: 2 Grace to you and peace from God our Father and the Lord Jesus Christ. 3 Blessed be the God and Father of our Lord Jesus Christ, who has blessed us in Christ with every spiritual blessing in the heavenly places. (Eph 1:1–3)

PAUL BEGINS HIS LETTER by saying that he was called and elected by God. Paul did not choose this himself but he was established as an apostle by the special will of God and a decree of God's providence. God called him to this apostolic state and established him in this foundation through faith. Because of this, Paul succeeds and bears spiritual fruit as an apostle. If someone tries to act on her own will and desires, she will not have success. Instead, God has given Paul the apostolic state with the grace and fruit that this state brings.

> Just as he chose us in him before the foundation of the world, that we should be holy and blameless before him in love. (Eph 1:4)

Here we see that God chooses and elects us before the creation of the world. Not only apostles are chosen, but God also chooses the faithful believers and makes them blameless before him. O God, you have the wonderful character of foreknowledge and perfect understanding! However, most people only reason about God from a human perspective and because of this they have only errors and misunderstandings about God. It is a strange thing that people who pride themselves on having justice misunderstand justice. They think God's justice should be as they think. They reason about God from a human perspective. O, we are so blind! One day we'll see the impenetrable depths of God's judgments and how His ways are known only to Him! What we now in our ignorance regard as an injustice of God will appear to us then as God's purest justice and strongest mercy.

> He destined us for adoption as his children through Jesus Christ, according to the good pleasure of his will, 6 to the praise of his glorious grace that he freely bestowed on us in the Beloved. (Eph 1:5–6)

O, God! We should melt in gratitude because of your pure goodness and mercy toward us. We have no merit in ourselves. With our effort, we can do nothing except evil. My God! In your goodness you chose us. But what did you choose us for? To be mediocre, common and ordinary? No, you chose us *to be your adopted children.* The only begotten Son of God, Jesus Christ, is infinite and all powerful. He loves us with his infinite love. Through his love, he makes us his adopted children.

We are adopted through the Son and in the Son. In our adoption the Holy Spirit moves into our lives and communicates to us the Son's Word. Jesus Christ testifies to this truth when he says, "He will glorify me, for he will take what is mine and declare it to you" (John 16:14). Through the Son's love, we pass into the Son and love because we are in the Son. In the Son we lose all complacency. This is why Paul writes that *he now lives in Jesus Christ who makes him strong.* Through the Son's adoption of him, Paul has passed into the Son. Only those within the Son can please the Son.

And the Son makes use of us to honor *the praise of His glorious grace.* So those who oppose living in the movement of the Spirit and oppose the transformation that the Word brings, oppose not only their own eternal happiness but oppose even more the glory of God. For us who believe, God gives us the Spirit of his Son to dwell inside of us and then we dwell in his Son. This is what Jesus Christ says in Revelation that all should hear that he is *the beginning and the end,* "I am the alpha and the omega" Revelation 1:8. The beginning is in creation when the Spirit of the Word inspired Adam. In redemption we live in the Word, so that the truth of redemption has its full effect on us, as long as we do not resist. Therefore, *the beginning* is when the Word lives in us and the *end* is when we live in the Son without which it is impossible to please God. Before the Word lives in us, we were hostile because of our sins. After we live in Christ, he makes us pleasing to Him and holds us in his loving gaze. Because the Son is the one who pleases God, we participate in the love between Father and the Son.

Paul supports what he says in Ephesians 1: 7–8 by what he has written in Romans 8:29, "For those whom he foreknew he also predestined to be conformed to the image of his Son, in order that he might be the firstborn within a large family." Paul became conformed to the Son by the Spirit of Jesus Christ living in him and then, living in the Son, he was born again. We also need for the Son to move into our hearts and then we move into the Son.

God gives himself in the economy of creation and redemption to place Spirit of the Word in all his people, to reproduce himself, so to speak, in humanity. God made human beings in the image of God and gives us his identity. God is pleased to remake us in his image by his Word by inviting us to live within him. O, adorable grandeur! O, the wonderful marvel that we discover in our interior! We receive this wisdom by dwelling within you! Paul describes the experience of all those who discover this wisdom within. If this wisdom is outside of ourselves, it appears foreign and strange to us but, if we pray even a little, wisdom comes within. We have light that is the light of God. Oh, then we discover, taste and feel the wonderful and glorious presence of God.

> In him we have redemption through his blood, the forgiveness of our trespasses, according to the riches of his grace 8 that he lavished upon us. (Eph 1:7)

But it was impossible after having sinned to return to the Word and pass into God again. We are no longer fully imprinted with the beautiful image of God given to us before the creation of the world. Our sins blotted out the image of God, that had expressed the Word in our Spirit, and now instead we had traces of the Devil. Without the character of God, a person cannot be received in the Word. Without the Word as our life's motivation and principle, we only struggle and subsist. Without a place in the Word, the person's place is in hell and life is one of sin.

So what does God do? God loves us with excessive goodness. This love does not follow ordinary rules of love that are grounded in reserve and prudence. O, God, you love with strength and without reservation! If we love with only ordinary wisdom and prudence, and if do not have innocent generosity and enthusiasm for your love, we cannot connect with the force and excess of your love for us! Therefore God places human beings in a place where they can find consummation through his abundant love. The Word reaches out and unites with us. And how does God do this? He pours out *his blood* that bathes and cleanses us, thus destroying the image of the devil. God is reestablished within. By this purification, the person finds salvation and lives within Jesus Christ.

Thus it is easy to see that the Word makes and operates salvation. The Word is the principle of creation and the way of redemption. In his glorification people reach their fulfillment and end.

Therefore, it is the blood of God shed so graciously that surpasses the grace of creation. Through his superabundant love, God puts love into us, filling us with true wisdom and prudence. This love between God and humanity is a love beyond anything else.

O, the mysteries of the Christian religion, that you are not known by all Christians! But why is it that you are not known? O, Jesus, why cannot I die a thousand times to make you known among human beings! Jesus Christ, you are not known among Christians. Actually God suffers less outrage from pagans and heretics from other religions than from Christians who have little knowledge and love for God. This makes many troubles. God suffers much pain from the idolatry of ignorant Christians. O, Christians, do you want to prevent all these misfortunes? Then, Christians, love and know Jesus Christ. You cannot love and know him without prayer, surrender, faith and love.

> He has made known to us the mystery of his will, according to his good pleasure that he set forth in Christ, 10 as a plan for the fullness of time, to gather up all things in him, things in heaven and things on earth. (Eph 1: 9)

My God! This Scripture is clear and transcendent. God works on behalf of humanity. God makes all things for the perfection and consummation of human beings. God plans for their joy and happiness by giving them the knowledge of the mystery of God's will and grace to follow this divine will always.

When the person loses her own will, she is placed in the essential will of God. Then nothing remains for the person on earth but to remain open, submerged and consummated in the will of God. The person never wants to leave.

It is appropriate that when the person begins to seek for union with God, she has to cross a desert and go through dreadful places. When the person arrives in God, she realizes that this is just a new beginning and she will go to a new infinite and immense home. The journey to God is a narrow but long way. The way takes her into in God's will where she moves already in eternity.

It is good when a person begins to do the will of God. Previously the person only did her will while believing that it was the will of God, but it was only the person's will.

When the person begins to do the will of God, she recognizes an unknown truth: God's infinity and eternity fulfill and consummate the person both now and forever. While close to the beginning of the spiritual journey, the person already has faith in the consummation but sees nothing with her eyes, yet in faith believes in the fulfillment. Later, after being led by God, the believer sees the way and the final destination, according to the measure of her advancement. If the person grows more, she sees that everything will be perfectly fulfilled and consummated, but this will take time. If the person is blessed to enter into God, she will soon be transformed.

Yet our sins can remove us from the way when we do not walk the right way because we do not follow the guidance of God.

We know that after a very long time, the believer finally arrives in peace if the person believes in consummation. Truly, this consummation brings about good and pure fulfillment. But we know that at the beginning of conversion, the person is not entirely consummated. It is then that the person discovers that in God there is an infinite country and that God always fulfills the person within the divine being and that throughout all eternity, the blessed will always be consummated in God in a wonderful way. This infinite consummation never exhausts eternity. Because God is infinite, eternity is endless. God communicates both eternity and infinity. If the believer reaches an end to their consummation, they would be like God and that is impossible.

Therefore I say that throughout eternity, the saints will be consumed more and more in God and discover throughout eternity inexpressible profundity of the divine. When the saints enter heaven, God makes them fully beatified and nothing could be added to their satisfaction. Because it is ineffable, they can never desire more consummation or any other thing, because they are perfectly transformed in the will of God.

Always we discover with an indescribable pleasure God's sweet kindness and the new profundity with which God ravishes us. Never throughout eternity can this be exhausted. We will always know and love God with growing passion. When we know and love God, we have the Word and the

Holy Spirit with us, and they show us how to increase our knowledge and love of God. As our loves increases, we are transformed, each according to his or her degree, into clarity upon clarity and love upon love.

This is the mystery and holiness of the will of God. Because of God's benevolence, it pleases him to make his will known to us. God decided this when he created us. O dignity! O grandeur! O the nobility of the Son of Man! You lost all these advantages for the dust of humanity that has only the small light of a torch. But when we lost the way to your kingdom, you came to us. Must we not admit that we are blind?

And through the holiness of God's will, you reunite us with the saints and unite us with the Word, who asks for our consummation in union. Jesus promises us, "I in them and you in me, that they may become completely one, so that the world may know that you sent me and loved them even as you loved me" (John 17:23). Jesus unites us with people and angels in God the Father. This union of mind and heart happens in this world and the next. This union also creates the miracle of union between a pastor and the church flock, such as between Paul and his flock.

> In Christ we have also obtained an inheritance, having been destined according to the purpose of him who accomplishes all things according to the counsel and will, 12 so that we, who were the first to hope on Christ, might live for the praise of his glory. (Eph 1:11–12)

The inheritance gives us the gift of dying with Christ and a reward for sharing his death with him. The inheritance given to us is to be *in Jesus*. It is in him that *we have been predestined* according to the will of God as a pure gift from his goodness. God has chosen these things according to his will and through pure mercy, *finally to the praise of his glory*. It is for his glory that we are chosen. We already hope in Jesus Christ and will be with him in eternity.

Paul says that God predestined us before the creation of the world. Following this, he says that we already hope in Jesus Christ and are to be to the praise of his glory. Paul speaks here as a Jew calling to Christians. To this he must distinguish two types of predestination. Our first predestination comes before creation as chosen to be conformed to the image of Jesus Christ. God created us for this fulfillment. The second predestination that Paul speaks about is the predestination for the reward of an inheritance.

The first predestination chooses us to be adopted children. The second gives us the inheritance of being the adopted child. This inheritance is given to us through grace and not because we deserved this. We have been adopted in Jesus Christ. This is what the Word inspires in us. This is the first predestination we had before the centuries but we were rendered unworthy of this adoption through the work of the devil who opposes our good Father. What does God do? Despite our predestination as children, we rejected him. Jesus Christ, in whom we have been predestined, reconciled us to God the Father and we enjoyed the new fruit of adoption. Next we obtain the inheritance.

This second predestination does not happen until we are reestablished and reconciled by Jesus Christ. As all our good graces and merits are in Jesus, also the reward and inheritance are fulfilled through the hope we have in Jesus Christ. The more we hope and trust in Jesus Christ, the more we find salvation and Jesus Christ works in our lives. We contemplate Jesus Christ without looking at anything else. Then we have more of the inheritance of Jesus Christ without planning for this inheritance. Only by hoping in Jesus Christ do we become conformed to him. This strong inheritance is filled with grandeur and plenty in proportion to the hope we have in Jesus Christ. These two predestinations are in the will of God, who makes all things according to the trust we have in his will and for his glory.

God makes nothing that is not for his glory and in his will we look at his glory. Through God's kindness, he allows us to see his glory. That is to say, God shows us his glory, so why do we sin? It is the will of sinners to dishonor God; the sinner attempts to dishonor, though God receives none of this. God shows his glory even in sins, but this does not hinder him from rigorously punishing sins. The sinner through malice wishes to dishonor God, yet God can never be dishonored. Everything sin does will bring eternal glory to God, even when the sinner is suffering in eternity.

> In him you also, when you had heard the word of truth, the gospel of your salvation, and had believed in him, were marked with the seal of the promised Holy Spirit; this is the pledge of our inheritance toward redemption of God's own people, to the praise of his glory. (Eph 1:13–14)

Here is the way God leads his people from the moment of their conversion until the moment of consummation. First, she *heard the word of truth*, and took it inside of herself, through the work of one of God's servants. This word is a word of life that convinces of sin, lies, and confusion. But with this comes power to hear the Word of life about *the path of salvation*, which is a change of heart. Following the reception of this light and knowledge, the soul through faith opens an interior door and flees away from what she acknowledges as evil. She embraces the good. After this, she is marked with *the seal* and grace is given to the soul. This grace is the *Holy Spirit*, through which the soul avoids evil and practices the good.

Secondly, this Holy Spirit works for the consummation of our soul. God gives us the Spirit and *pledges to us our inheritance* that we receive from *Christ's redemption*, according to our destiny. Paul describes how the redemption impacts both individuals and the universe, and eventually brings the consummation of Jesus Christ. Then all humanity will *praise Christ's glory*.

What does it mean to *praise the glory of God*? This is when the person is entirely detached from self-interest and fears neither honor nor dishonor. There is no concern about human appearances. Because of the Holy Spirit within, when disasters happen, she is still only concerned in the glory of God. Even in extreme misery and frightful misfortunes, she looks only at the glory of God and sings praises to the glory of God in the midst of ordeals. She knows that God is glorified in her ordeal and this glory of God creates joy and praises within her.

> I have heard of your faith in the Lord Jesus and your love toward all the saints, and for reason 16 I do not cease to give thanks for you as I remember you in my prayers. 17 I pray that the God of our Lord Jesus Christ, the Father of glory, may give you a spirit of wisdom and revelation as you come to know him. (Eph 1:15–17)

When Paul speaks *revelation*, he does not speak of extraordinary revelations and visions. These things must be received with humility without demanding them. The one entirely good and safe revelation is the revelation of our Lord Jesus Christ manifested in our soul. The person then enters into the knowledge of Jesus Christ by the experience of this state. Paul speaks of this revelation here. He addresses these faithful souls who are already filled with abundant love and prays this grace of all graces upon them, as a consummation of the grace, favor, and revelation of Jesus Christ. Paul prays for grace for them that prepares the soul for this manifestation of Jesus Christ.

> So that, with the eyes of your heart enlightened, you may know what is the hope to which he has called you, what are the riches of his glorious inheritance among the saints. (Eph 1:18)

My God! What good is said here! He enlightens the eyes of our heart, because it is the heart that tastes and experiences these things. We have a permanent and durable revelation of Jesus Christ, and, as he says, this enlightens the eyes of our heart.

But, O Paul, what are the eyes of the heart? The heart is blind and sees nothing.

The great Apostle answers, the eyes of the heart with the Spirit have great understanding. The heart without the spirit misunderstands and misinterprets experience.

Therefore, these eyes with the Spirit are the ones that Paul wishes for the Ephesians, that they may have the knowledge of the Lord. Paul writes, "You may know what is the hope to which he has called you." We are called to hope for the enjoyment of the Lord. This enjoyment underlies all of our experience, as if we were given a taste for an exquisite thing that was promised to us; to desire this is a great advantage. That we can conceive of this shows we must possess it. And then Paul adds that we can taste this hope for the "riches of his glorious inheritance among the saints." He speaks of the two inheritances, the one of God in the saints, and the other of saints in God. The goodness of God is so grand that he gives the inheritance to the saints, who are his adopted children, and, secondly, he wants the saints for his own inheritance. The same applies to the saints who receive the riches of his glory for their inheritance and give themselves to God for his inheritance. These two ways are written about in the Scripture, where, in one God calls Israel for his inheritance. "For you have separated them from among all the peoples of the earth, to be your heritage, just as you promised through Moses, your servant, when you brought our ancestors out of Egypt, O Lord God" (1 Kgs 8:53). And another Scripture reads, "I will gather all the nations and bring them down to the valley of Jehosphatat, and I will enter judgment with them there, on account of my people and my heritage Israel, because they have scattered them among the nations" (Joel 3:2). Also in Psalm 16:5–6, David says, "The Lord is my chosen portion and my cup; you hold my lot. The boundary lines have fallen for me in pleasant places; I have a goodly heritage." In Jesus Christ, human beings become the inheritance of God, as God wants to be the inheritance of human beings. My God, your goodness is wonderful!

> And what is the immeasurable greatness of his power for us who believe, according to the working of his great power. 20 God put this power to work in Christ when he raised him from the dead and seated him at his right hand in the heavenly places. (Eph 1:19–20)

These expressions Paul uses are very beautiful and strong! It is true, O my God! You appear in favor to those who are elected and chosen to enjoy you in *the greatness of your power,* goodness and magnificence. You use your power on behalf of souls who have faith and trust in your supreme power. Those who want worldly power and defy the divine power are indignant at those who receive divine power.

Yet faithful people believe even when there is no reason to believe, who hope against all expectations, and who see into the profound depths of God. Truthfully, they believe without hesitation or do not doubt that God will act. They feel well the efficacy of the virtues. The divine power grounds the faithful.

But we might say, I do not doubt the divine power, but I doubt that God will use his power for me because of my unworthiness. Yet, God does not regard our worthiness or unworthiness, but only regards his will. His power always follows his will. Because of this, there is no reason to doubt. He will exercise his power perfectly for us and his will shows his favor for us. I abandon myself entirely to God's will who gives us an excellent conformity to his divine will.

One may make this objection. Why does not everyone sense the great richness of the divine power, our God who likes to appear in impossible places? It is because they either do not have sufficient faith in his power or they oppose his power.

When has God shown his strength? We see God's power in the resurrection of Jesus Christ and in his eternal establishment of Jesus Christ at his right hand as our Mediator. God also resurrects us and calls us to be in Jesus Christ through Christ's hypostatic union. Christ unites human nature with the Word and raises us to the right hand of God above everything else.

> Far above all rule and authority and power and dominion, and above every name that is named, not only in this age but also in the age to come. 22 And he has put all things under his feet and has made him the head over all things for the church, 23 which is his body, the fullness of him who fills all in all. (Eph 1: 21–23)

Jesus Christ has raised human nature above the state of angels. Jesus Christ is above all that is and all that is possible, except for that reserved for God. Everything is subject to Jesus Christ. If he is raised above the angels, he is raised above all that is on the earth. There is nothing greater on earth than his church, and God has established Christ as its head.

This church is Christ's body and his fullness, that is to say, as his natural body found fullness in its hypostatic union, where the fullness of God is communicated. Also, as Christ is the mystical body, we find fullness in union with all its members. His fullness fills and consummates the church in general and its members in particular. When this happens, the church accomplishes his will and works for human fulfillment.

> You were dead through the trespasses and sins 2 in which you once lived, following the course of this world, following the ruler of the power of the air, the spirit that is now at work among those who are disobedient. 3 All of us once lived among them in the passions of our flesh, following the desires of flesh and senses, and we were by nature children of wrath, like everyone else. 4 But God, who is rich in mercy, out of the great love with which he loved us 5 even when we were dead through our trespass, made us alive together with Christ—by grace you have been saved. (Eph 2:1–5)

Paul speaks here of the first state when we were converted to help us see that we have been criminals worthy of God's anger and unworthy of his mercy, yet God gives us his infinite mercy. God gives us life when we were dead through trespasses and sins because of our crimes, committed when we were filled with passion and self-love, a state entirely opposed to Jesus Christ. When we turn to him, he frees us of our own desires and gives us a new life that is filled with grace. Truly God offers infinite mercy and reconciliation to sinners. He becomes our friend. The prophet Zechariah says that we are the apple of God's eye (Zech 2:8). We are deeply cherished in Jesus Christ. It is not difficult to understand that with love like this, God gave us his only Son to save us.

For me, I am greatly astonished, when I see Christians that are ignorant that Jesus Christ is the Word, the only Son of the Father, and that Jesus Christ died to give us life. God can give souls the great gift of being united to him. And isn't it folly to doubt this grace, after we have received so much? Because finally, union between our soul and God puts things right, according to the order of creation. God gives us participation in his being to restore us to our original state of being. The goal and purpose of God's glory is that we enjoy him and unite with His Word. God desires to encounter us and become one. This is the grace of righteousness, according to the order of creation. This is the way God leads souls so we arrive at union with him and nothing surpasses this. But God, who loved his Son, delivered him to death for us who abuse his grace and mercy; truly the

Son was given for our offenses. This is astonishing love. This is why Paul writes in Romans, "He who did not withhold his own Son, but gave him up for all of us, will he not with him also give us everything else?" (Romans 8:32). Otherwise, we ignore Jesus Christ and the profound and wonderful mysteries of our religion. Instead of faithful people, we become like parrots who do not understand what they are taught and only repeat things. We should have our foundation on the mysteries of our religion. As we deepen our understanding, it becomes impossible that we can doubt what we have. Sadly though, some see union with God as extraordinary, perilous, and dangerous! It is not extraordinary because it is the goal of creation and the fruit of redemption. It is not perilous, because it is our destiny. The extraordinary part is that Jesus Christ dies for ungrateful people such as us and that his Father gave him for our salvation.

If we comprehend this, we arrive at union with him because he calls us to him. It is easy to arrive since Jesus Christ in Revelation invites all Christians to come. "The Spirit and the bride say, 'Come.' And let everyone who hears say, 'Come.' And let everyone who is thirsty come" (Rev 22:17). He says, "Let anyone who wishes take the water of life as a gift." He also says, "Therefore I counsel you to buy from me gold refined by fire so that you may be rich" (Rev 3:18). Also, "Ho, everyone who thirsts, come to the waters; and you that have no money, come, buy and eat!" (Isa 55:1).

Paul is direct with these Christians in Ephesus about this interior grace to which they are called, as he writes in this first chapter. He tells them about the first mercy of God given to them, they may with confidence hope for the second mercy of consummation. He then offers the apostles and himself as examples of those who had been sinners (as were those in Ephesus) and yet have reached such a great blessing. This is why the Ephesians must hope after having seen God's mercy given to the others.

> And raised us up with him and seated us with him in the heavenly places in Christ Jesus, 7 so that in the ages to come he might show the immeasurable riches of his grace in kindness toward us in Christ Jesus. (Eph 2: 6–7)

Paul adds something he has not said before about the mystical resurrection and the soul's establishment in the repose of permanent union. Nothing is more consoling than this. He assures us that we are raised by the same *God who raised Jesus Christ*. We pass through the death of Adam to the life of Jesus Christ: we are not content to live the hard life of propriety, but we are given the new life of Jesus Christ. Even more, we are *seated with him in the heavenly places.* That is to say, we have passed into Jesus Christ who now lives in us. In God we dwell in a perfect repose. The Word *sitting in God* marks our permanent and durable repose.

This is to say that God *will show in the coming centuries the immeasurable richness of his grace* and his kindness. But how, O apostles, will God show his abundant richness of grace and kindness toward us? Will it be in his union with us? Truly, Jesus Christ's grace is exceedingly for us poor creatures. Paul tells us that out of his infinite goodness Jesus Christ died for us so that we might live in his great goodness. Here, says Paul, we will be seated throughout eternity in heaven with the saints and their profound recollection. We will have the sight of the incomprehensible mystery. This Angel Satan was there when God said that human beings could be united with him through eternity and that this would be a joy to share with them. The angels were surprised to see ungrateful people abusing such a singular grace: God gave his own Son and he died to save people. Satan and some of the angels refused to submit to the Son of God and revolted against him. But yet they were surely surprised when their rebellion and revolt multiplied, and they fell. In their extreme sin, they fell into evil.

Therefore, I say following Paul, that the greatest astonishment in human history is the mercy that God has in Jesus Christ who gives to humanity the graces of his holy glory. God gives us consummation of graces, such as described in the Beatitudes. God gives blessings, joy and glory to us. In giving his Son and through the annihilation of his death, God brings fulfillment. As Paul writes that Christ Jesus "did not regard equality with God as something to be exploited, but emptied himself, taking the form of a slave, being born in human likeness" (Phil 2:6–7). God gives us these understandings.

> For by grace you have been saved through faith, and this is not your own doing; it is the gift of God. (Eph 2:8)

After Paul shows us the glory of Jesus Christ's salvation, he reveals to us how God gives us salvation. We glorify him because of this gift! God gives us salvation through his superabundant mercy and not through any merit on our part. It is *through faith that we are saved* and this faith is a *gift of God.* We have made nothing, but we receive everything through grace, including the works he has prepared for us to walk in. Can anyone create a good work without grace? The works might themselves be good, but are useless when destitute of grace. What do we glorify without grace? Nothing.

We have no works without faith and grace. Our efforts are all futile in themselves. Vainly do our efforts try to get this grace. Our strength is blind! Yet Jesus Christ gives grace to those who ask for his will. Jesus Christ asks nothing of us except that we ask. His will itself is grace and he gives to those who ask.

Yet some refuse grace. The immoral person says, "I won't accept this, if something is given to me to do." O libertine! You take pleasure that you refuse God. How frequently is this grace offered and you do not receive it? You want things only through your own efforts. You like your excess. Yet grace is so close that it waits at the door Revelation 3:20 reads, "Listen! I am standing at the door, knocking; if you hear my voice and open the door, I will come in to you and eat with you, and you with me."

Jesus Christ watches every morning. All we must do is open the door. *We are all created in Jesus Christ.* It is pure grace that we have been created and regenerated in him. God has prepared good works for us and creates salvation for us. Sadly in our freedom we have rebelled and we lose both Christ's way and the end.

In our thirst, we have before us the water. All we have to do is to lower ourselves to drink, yet we do not do this. There is a world of difference between our salvation and our loss. Our salvation comes from God, but our loss comes from ourselves because we refuse the ways of salvation. When we accept God's ways, we are not glorified ourselves. God wills that we offer ourselves and become full of gratitude. Without this, we lose our freedom because we refuse the way of salvation.

> So then, remember that at one time you Gentiles by birth, called "the uncircumcision" by those who are called "the circumcision"— a physical circumcision made in the flesh by human hands. (Eph 2:11)

Paul reminds us of the deplorable state we were in before God's mercy found us so we are filled with gratitude. We know because we are the recipients of mercy that we need *the blood of Jesus Christ.* Our gratitude opens us for the outpouring of the blood of Jesus Christ.

This truth enlightens our souls, filling us with all the graces of Jesus Christ. We understand how great it is that God gave us Jesus Christ. This singular grace, the source of all other graces, makes us melt in love for God's grace. O, gift of Jesus Christ! You are not understood and respected, because the leaders do not know you. O, grandeur of the Christian faith through which the gift is given, you are wonderful! O, Christian, know the grandeur and the name of Christ! How much this cost Christ! Through God's invisible hand, Jesus Christ reaches down to us! O, gift that surpasses all other gifts! O, goodness of the giver, the greatness of which a poor heart cannot carry unless you carry the weight yourself. Only God can support the favors of God. All other favors are nothing in light of this favor of God. O, Christian faith, we wish you known through the world!

> For he is our peace; in his flesh he has made both groups into one and has broken down the dividing wall, that is, the hostility between us. 15 He has abolished the law with its commandments and ordinances, that he might create in himself one new humanity in place of the two, thus making peace, 16 and might reconcile both groups to God in one body through the cross, thus putting to death that hostility through it. (Eph 2:14–16)

Jesus Christ is *our peace and our reconciliation* with his Father. Christ establishes us in God in a permanent peace. He places the peace within us, and communicates to us the Holy Spirit. Therefore, through his divine Word he unites the faithful with the unfaithful, the just with the unjust. Christ banishes the unfaithfulness from the unfaithful, the injustice from the unjust to create a perfect unity. All the different nations will be consummated in union. He has broken down all obstacles that prevent a perfect union. He broke the cause of division through his reconciliation, making everything into one union. God alone unites the heart and the Spirit. He unites our exterior lives through his cross into one body living the same faith and practicing the same laws.

> So he came and preached peace to you who were far off and peace to those who were near; 18 for through him both of us have access in one Spirit to the Father. (Eph 2:17–18)

This confirms beautifully how Jesus Christ came to announce peace to everyone and to make peace between us. He approached those who were far off and gives them the same access to the Father. Jesus Christ reunites us with his Father and also perfectly unites us together through the communication of his Spirit. This unity of the Spirit makes a union of the heart. What greater unity is there than to have the same spirit, the Spirit of the Word?

> So then you are no longer strangers and aliens, but you are citizens with the saints and also members of the household of God, 20 built upon the foundation of the apostles and prophets, with Christ Jesus himself as the cornerstone. 21 In him the whole structure is

joined together and grows into a holy temple in the Lord; 22 in whom you also are being built together spiritually into a dwelling place for God. (Eph 2:19–22)

In this passage Paul tells us that in Jesus Christ we have the wonderful advantage of being reunited with God as pure children. He makes us into a temple of the Lord where God lives in our interior. Faithful believers do not have a separate and distinct temple but share one temple with one Spirit, heart and body in which God lives by His Holy and Indivisible Spirit.

The temple of his body is composed of many Christians who are filled with Jesus Christ. The chisel of suffering made these Christians into the polished stones of this wonderful edifice. This temple grows and changes until all new Christians return to it. As the interior temple grows in each person until its consummation, so the general temple increases as founded by the apostles and prophets on the very foundation of Jesus Christ. The same Spirit is all in all, both in the general and the particular, as they become united.

> This is the reason I Paul am a prisoner for Christ Jesus for the sake of you Gentiles—2 for surely you have already heard of the commission of God's grace that was given me for you, 3 and how the mystery was made known to me by revelation, as I wrote above in a few words, 4 a reading of which will enable you to perceive my understanding of the mystery of Christ. (Eph 3:1–4)

An apostle is frequently a *prisoner for his disciples*. Paul is not speaking of a material prison but an interior prison in which God places the apostolic soul. The apostle pays with exactitude for his children of grace and, in doing so, truly imitates Jesus Christ. The apostle pays what he does not owe and bears the sins he has not committed. God regards these apostolic souls and makes them pay the debts of others because of love and bear the sins they have not committed. This gives them knowledge of what Jesus Christ has suffered for them.

Paul shows us the plan of grace given by the Father to Jesus Christ and then revealed to us. For as Jesus Christ carries our burdens to the Father, on Earth the apostles delight in bearing the burdens of others. These fathers and mothers of grace also carry other souls and their burdens to Jesus Christ. Paul tells us of this admirable plan of grace.

Paul assures us about the grace of *the mystery of Jesus Christ* and the two mysteries of the pastoral office. In the first mystery of the pastoral office, the pastor brings back the lost sheep to the flock of Jesus Christ and puts them on the shoulders of Jesus Christ. As the pastor knows, the sheep need to go to Jesus Christ and not to propriety.

After the pastor brings the sheep to Jesus Christ, what happens next? In the second mystery of the pastoral office, the pastor then leaves the soul there to discover and know Jesus Christ. We need to know with passion Jesus Christ and through him the Father. Jesus Christ makes known to us this supreme grace of graces. All the other graces are nothing compared to this. This is what Paul calls a revealed mystery: the revelation of Jesus Christ, whose manifestation is given according to the degree and capacity of the soul. This comes from on high and is the revelation of revelations.

> In former generations this mystery was not made known to humankind, as it has now been revealed to his holy apostles and prophets by the Spirit: that is, the Gentiles have become fellow heirs, members of the same body, and sharers in the promise in Christ Jesus through the gospel. (Eph 3:5–6)

Jesus Christ was not manifested or discovered in the old Law but in the new Gospel. Although the saints of old participated in the same Jesus Christ, he was not revealed to them in the same depth of revelation of which Paul writes. In the Old Testament, Jesus Christ is most clearly revealed in David. Jesus Christ had given a strong manifestation of himself as Prophet-King to David. David was truly a figure of Jesus Christ, because David did not do the will of people like Saul did. Instead, David chose to do the will of God. As it says in 1 Samuel 13:14 and Acts 13:22, David was a man following God's own heart. It is certain that David is the true revelation of Jesus Christ, and that in David and his life is seen imprinted the image of Jesus Christ.

The second thing that is revealed in the new time that was not revealed before is the *reunion of all people* in Jesus Christ. Paul writes that the Jews will be reunited with the Gentiles. David had this same revelation, as written about in the Psalms, prophets, and Isaiah, to whom Jesus Christ was revealed. Paul does not speak in particular of these holy prophets, but this puts in perspective the work of the apostles in bringing together these two groups of people. The Messiah Jesus Christ brings the manifestation and knowledge of God to people who do not have him. Paul writes of the consummation of all the people in Jesus Christ in one spirit. According to the apostle Paul, Jesus Christ is formed in our interior life.

> Of this gospel I have become a servant according to the gift of
> God's grace that was given me by the working of his power. 8 Al-
> though I am the very least of all the saints, this grace was given
> to me to bring to the Gentiles the news of the boundless riches of
> Christ, and to make everyone see what is the plan of the mystery
> hidden for ages in God who created all things. (Eph 3:7–9)

Paul speaks here of the two hidden but real graces given to us. The first
grace is the gift of the revelation of Jesus Christ. This grace manifested Jesus
Christ to Paul, the least of all the apostles. This grace humbles and brings
truth that forms the Word within the interior life. God takes pleasure in
choosing this apostle and forming his exterior ministry and interior Word.

As faithful Christians, God gives us love for these leaders, because if
we love Jesus Christ, we will love Paul and David. Jesus Christ made David
the pastor of Israel. Jesus Christ also made Paul the pastor of the Gentiles.
In their lives they were faithful imitators of Jesus Christ.

Paul describes the graces given to us. By grace, Jesus Christ lives
within us. By grace, Jesus Christ also marks and claims our exterior life.
In this way, Jesus Christ manifested himself in Paul and Paul became part
of Christ, the Beloved. Song of Solomon 5:16 reads, "This is my beloved
and this is my friend, O daughters of Jerusalem." O, that grace lives in the
interior of Paul, so we see him in Jesus Christ! Secondly, Jesus Christ also
gives Paul the grace of caring for his flock.

Paul describes this interior grace as the manifestation of Jesus Christ
in the heart, a reality profound and admirable. This manifestation of Jesus
Christ comes from on high to impress the manifestation in our interior.
This is *the mystery hidden in God before all ages* because God created the
world for this manifestation of Jesus Christ. Through him and for him, all
people have been created. Through him and for him, all people have been
redeemed. Through him and for him, all people have been glorified. Therefore, this manifestation is the mystery of creation, redemption, and glorification. Through the operations of the three divine persons, all are made
in Jesus Christ and through Jesus Christ, as we are assured by John 1:3 "All
things came into being through him, and without him not one thing came
into being." The Father created humanity in his Son and for his Son. We
receive the Spirit of the Son to renew the image of the Son, as we wait for
the second coming of the Son.

And there could be no other purpose in the creation of the world than
to extend Jesus Christ to humanity so they become infinite in him because

humanity is completed in him. Because the generation of the Word is infinite, the Word being as infinite as the Father, all goes into the same infinity. It is impossible that there are more than three persons in the Trinity because what is received is infinitely making infinity and infinity is inexhaustible which means that it is incessantly creating, flowing into the Word and communicating this to us. This makes an immense and equal movement uniting people to the Father and to the Son; their unity does not surpass the Word. The Father begets the Son. The Father and the Son have their ineffable relationship and commerce one with another so that the Word may pass into all people in order to receive the Trinity and to make a constant flow into them. This is like a stream of water flowing from a source into a meadow without ceasing and without danger.

Therefore I say that this flow of divinity, that is a livening principle, could not come except through the Word because the flow from the Father goes into strong souls more or less according to their capacity and extension, that the flow is received, remade and returned to the unity. The Holy Spirit glorifies Christ who unites us with him in eternity. The Holy Spirit glorifies us through Jesus Christ and for Jesus Christ, according to the capacity given to us to receive Jesus Christ. The Spirit transforms people in creation; this is the same Spirit that is in Jesus Christ. Jesus Christ himself has said,

> When the Spirit of truth comes, he will guide you into all the truth; for he will not speak on his own, but will speak whatever he hears, and he will declare to you the things that are to come. All the Father has is mine. For this reason I said that he will take what is mine and declare it to you. (John 16: 13–15)

In the mystery of the Incarnation, which is also the mystery of our sanctification, the Holy Spirit forms the body of Jesus Christ within us in mystery through the Word and by the Word. Through the life-giving Word, the Holy Spirit also puts the Word within Mary. All of the operations of the Holy Spirit have this as its goal: the formation of Jesus Christ within us.

All the operations of the Trinity, even in the outside world, are intended to create Jesus Christ within us. Therefore this is *the mystery hidden in the ages*. Also, in the Trinity the eternal occupation of the Father creates his Word and the occupation of the Holy Spirit engenders the reception of the Word. The mutual love of the Father and the Son and the Holy Spirit flow among them. As the Son receives the Father, the Word flows everywhere through the work of the Holy Spirit. Losing ourselves in infinite love, we receive new knowledge and love. O Truth! O Grandeur! O immensity that science may not discover, but is discovered in this same immensity!

> So that through the church the wisdom of God in its rich variety might now be made known to the rulers and authorities in the heavenly places. 11 This was in accordance with the eternal purpose that he has carried out in Christ Jesus our Lord, 12 in whom we have access to God in boldness and confidence through faith in him. 13 I pray therefore that you may not lose heart over my sufferings for you; they are your glory. (Eph 3:10–13)

After Paul declares the mystery hidden in God that is the manifestation of Jesus Christ, he writes about the ways in which God is pleased to manifest Jesus Christ. The ways are *known to principalities and powers in heaven* and fill us with delight and joy. They replenish us also with contentment which God takes pleasure in manifesting.

This admirable economy *of the wisdom of God* is seen in Jesus Christ and in his church. Jesus Christ manifests himself in the church. This manifestation gives us the knowledge of God in his church and in particular souls.

What manifestation is the church given? The manifestation of Jesus Christ gives us *freedom to speak to God and to approach God with confidence*. This way pleasing to God is given to us through faith. Jesus Christ gives us the ability to approach God with faith and confidence; to hold on to him; to remain in his presence; and to listen. The church that practices this speaks with God, listens, and obeys. Always in his presence, the church loves confidently. Jesus Christ merits and manifests this grace for us.

From this we can infer that prayer is necessary. We can do nothing without prayer. Prayer is the way Jesus Christ communicates and manifests himself to us.

The cross always accompanies prayer. That is why Paul produced spiritual children by the cross. The cross and prayer are companions. Nothing is done in redemption except by the cross and prayer of Jesus Christ. Also, nothing is done in particular souls, in the church, except through prayer and the cross. Prayer and the cross create children for Jesus Christ.

This is why Paul *prays* that the Ephesians *not lose heart over what he is suffering for them*. Without suffering one cannot believe and bring forth souls for Jesus Christ. As we know, Jesus Christ suffered for our redemption.

But out of Jesus Christ's sorrows and suffering came the glories and well-being of Christians. In a similar fashion, the sufferings of grace-filled fathers and mothers brings *the glory and the well-being* of their children. This is why Paul beseeches his dear children not to be discouraged because of what he suffers at this time. In fact, they must take new courage because his suffering brings the mercy that Jesus Christ gives them. This is why his suffering brings mercy and a shower of refreshment for his children.

It is not that fathers have merit in themselves to serve for the sanctification of others. Oh, no. All the merit is contained in Jesus Christ and received by the grandest of saints who dwell in pure nothingness. Without faith, how can we do anything for others? But through Jesus Christ's merits and suffering, grace extends to these fathers and mothers this merit for the salvation and perfection of their children. Jesus Christ extends the benefits of his passion to all his children. Paul offers Christ's merits to all church members when he says, "I am completing what is lacking in Christ's afflictions for the sake of his body, that is, the church" (Col 1:24). As he says, he extends and offers Christ's merits to the faithful. Paul's sufferings are an extension of those of Jesus Christ, and have an admirable efficacy to produce souls in Jesus Christ.

This is the admirable secret that is discovered. As a man, Jesus Christ's sufferings brought merit and glory for human nature. As Jesus Christ said speaking of his human nature said that it was necessary that "the Son of Man must undergo great suffering" (Luke 9:22) and enter into his glory. Meaning that for his sufferings to cause hypostatic union between the human and the infinite divine, he must acquire for himself an infinite merit. But beyond personal merit, he has merited this for humanity with superabundance, but also for all possible worlds. Jesus Christ takes pleasure in extending the merits of his sufferings to his members. Finally, to receive this, we know we must go to Jesus Christ, and accept in our sincere heart his communication to us.

If we leave the light of wisdom that God gives his church, we wander alone as poor children. Even though our Lord reaches out to us, we might not have comprehended these blessings and merits. Jesus Christ is our mediator without sin. All mediation is contained in him and he has pleasure in extending this mediation to the saints. This serves our Lord's glory and takes nothing away from him. It pleases the Father that through his Son the Spirit flows to all humanity. Yet this does not diminish the grandeur of the Word and the Word always remains whole and in the same bosom of the Father. This offering of the Trinity serves only to give to the Trinity the full glory that the saints also knew. Because of the merits of Jesus Christ, believers receive a personal merit appropriate to them. We lose ourselves in the infinite merits of Jesus Christ. Jesus Christ continually renews and perpetuates his sacrifice on the Cross. This increases both glory to God and benefits to humanity.

Some out of malice invent errors about this. They are ignorant of the mysteries of our religion and the pure belief of our church. This happens because almost no pastors are both learned and active in prayer. Lord, give to your church pastors who are both learned and interior.

> For this reason I bow my knees before the Father, 15 from whom every family in heaven and on earth takes its name. 16 I pray that according to the riches of his glory, he may grant that you be strengthened in your inner being with power through his Spirit. (Eph 3:14–16)

This is what Paul calls to *bow the knee*, which is to act in surrender and annihilation before the majesty of God, by which he acknowledges that God is the father who makes him an apostle. Through his apostolate, he was made a father of an infinite number of Christians. But he attributes nothing to his paternity, but sees only God as his origin. This is why, he says, "I bow my knees." This is to say, I abandon myself to God the Father, and God has given me authority over you. I am your father on earth like he is your father in heaven. I see in Jesus Christ all the families and all the children are in Jesus Christ and all the fathers are given through Jesus Christ. All originate in God the Father. Paul claims no rights of authority for himself.

The riches of his glory annihilates us, so that he may grant strength in our inner being with power through his Spirit. All that an apostle may desire is to have their children fortified in their interior being and that God may give grace to their interior of his Spirit. When the Spirit of the divine filiation, for whom we cry, "Abba, our Father!" spreads through our hearts, we have the interior Spirit, which is none other than that of Jesus Christ, by whom we are adopted. The Spirit unites us with God. Through God we become united with all our brothers and sisters to make a perfect union. This Spirit makes us close with God, so that we may hold on to his presence and speak with him. Finally we may unite with him.

And that Christ may dwell in our hearts through faith. (Eph 3:17)

This interior Spirit is no other than the spirit of *faith*, of which has frequently been spoken, by which *Jesus Christ lives truthfully in our heart*. This is not a transitory union, but Christ living permanently within us. This

Spirit of faith makes the soul bypass any light in the abyss except sacred darkness of the faith. The soul finds this uncreated light and writes, "He made darkness his covering around him, his canopy thick clouds dark with water" (Ps 18:11) because the soul perceives the darkness and yet the increasing divine light is hidden in the darkness. This light is Jesus Christ's splendor shining on the saints. The soul is astonished by the power of faith leading in the darkness in an unknown country, where she spends long years without knowledge. She finds Jesus Christ hidden in this darkness, who appears when we least expect him.

> As you are being rooted and grounded in love. 18 I pray that you
> may have the power to comprehend, with all the saints, what is the
> breadth and length and height and depth. (Eph 3:17b–18)

When the soul arrives in God by the way of faith, than Jesus Christ is manifested, and when Jesus Christ is manifested, the soul is strengthened and grounded in a pure, perfect, and durable love.

This perfect love unites with faith and hope in a wonderful unity as if in an abyss. This love gives the person the knowledge of *the breadth and length and height and depth*, in the infinite abyss of the immensity of the Trinity. The Son contains the profundity and immensity of the Trinity because Jesus Christ is the breadth and length and height and depth of the Father. He is the height since he is the glory. He is the depth because he has the wisdom of God, the secret of the depths, and complete access to the depths of God. Even more, the depths flow in him that is the immensity of the Father. Because the Father lives in him, infinity flows into infinity and always will flow into one another. Because the Father begets the Son, nothing is hidden from the Word, nothing is lost and the Word gives everything to the Father that is given to him and Father returns everything to him.

As the Father loses nothing of who he is, neither does the Son. The Father remains as immense God, the Son has the immensity of God, and the Holy Spirit has the immensity of God. All is together reduced into unity, where the Father and the Son and the Holy Spirit all give and receive; this is found in unity. In every moment the Father engenders his Word as a way of knowledge, that is to say, he communicates all that he is through the Spirit without holding anything in reserve. The Son engenders love for his Father, as he loves the Father and engenders love. The Father reciprocates the Son's love and the Son produces the Spirit and there is no division and the Trinity is always a unity, yet nothing is lost in this unity. Their action is never interrupted. Their repose never stops, a fertile repose that is the conduit for repose, and that is lost in the same repose. O adorable God, you are here! Your impenetrable profundity has all that you are so it pleases you to manifest yourself to your saints through Jesus Christ, who is the one that knows all your profundity and dimensions, and also the one who makes this known.

We see in Jesus Christ the height, depth, length, and breadth of the Father's love. Height is the divinity. The depth is the annihilation. The breadth is the extent of his love. The length is his extreme patience. He has given all on the cross, where he was raised on high, which is the mark of the height of his Divinity. His feet walk the earth showing the profound abasement when he allowed himself to be reduced to union with human nature. His arms are extended which is the mark of his extreme love that made him embrace all humanity and bear all their sins and problems on his infinite merit. His patience supports their ingratitude.

The height, length, breadth and depth of the Trinity and of Jesus Christ will be the joy and the pleasure that the saints will have throughout eternity because all through eternity their understanding will deepen, and they will discover new beauty that never ends.

> And to know the love of Christ that surpasses knowledge, so that
> you may be filled with all the fullness of God. (Eph 3:19)

There are two things that are immense, infinite, incomprehensible, and that may never fully be discovered: the immensity of God and the infinite love of Jesus Christ for people. The Trinity's love surpasses all that may be thought. For this love we should die a thousand times with love and gratitude. This incomprehensible and infinite love surpasses all the external testimonials given to it because what he had inside was still more than appeared on the outside. This is why after having given his blood and his life for human beings, as if his love was only satisfied by this sacrifice, he opens the heart of human beings, to behold the depths of his extreme love. He speaks to them about how his testimony needs to be radical in order to express his love and to satisfy our hearts. This is why Christ gave all, to satisfy this love, so that we are filled with his love and we return this same love to him. This is a mystery that he reveals. Because of love, Jesus Christ opened his heart and gave us a home. O love, you answered with the blood and life of God! You opened your heart, the seat of love, so that you can pour on humanity your infinite love. By doing this, you receive humanity within you, and we live. Christ gives all through love, and this same love gives us faith. It was not enough to give the blood from his veins; indeed, he gives the blood from his heart. This love exhausted all that was in the body of Jesus Christ. Through the profound opening in his heart, out flowed his blood and water. This water and blood was the sign that his love had given all. O people, if you discover the extreme love in the heart of Jesus, this is the door. His heart was reduced to dust but his love made it a diamond.

Ultimately, why did Jesus Christ pour out his love? He sent out uncreated love, the Holy Spirit. Only to give love can satisfy this love of God. Paul writes this to us: the love of Jesus Christ presses on us! O love, incomprehensible love! This allows you to work in our hearts!

Therefore, the love of Jesus Christ has ransomed us and purified us through his blood. We are willing to be freed from our sins that operate in us.

By Christ's annihilation, we receive the fullness of God. Christ opens his heart to communicate to people the fullness of Divinity! My God! That humanity is called to such high things!

However, people do not know and they amuse themselves with trifles. Then they lose these immense treasures and the infinite richness of the love of God for humanity.

> Now to him who by the power at work within us is able to accomplish abundantly for more than all we can ask or imagine, 21 to him be glory in the church and in Christ Jesus to all generations, forever and ever. Amen. (Eph 3:20–21)

My God! We are foolish to limit our prayers and ask only certain limited things with a certain grace. It seems to me that this is treating God as a human being and we ask much less than God wants to give and, indeed, what God does give. It is like asking a king for only a penny. We should not conform our requests to what we want, but our requests should reflect the grandeur and the magnificence of the giver. If we rely on the will of the King, and ask only for our necessities, we lose the real treasure. The true request is that we ask nothing of God except to accomplish his holy will. We ask this of the Father and abandon to him all the rest. O, he gives us *good better than all that we can ask or desire, or even imagine!* Who could ever think of the mercies that God makes for souls, and imagine them, far from asking for them? It is impossible. When the holy Patriarchs desire the Messiah with all their heart, they asked for both a Savior and King. But after the Savior of Israel came, he was hung on a tree in disgrace, and they committed parricide. This thought alone would have filled them with horror.

Therefore, it is necessary to remain in God who works in us with efficacy. Paul says, God operates more than a thousand times better than we can think. My God, we are blind to the actions of Your will acting for us and operating within us. Instead of ever leaving him, we should remain and let Jesus Christ act and operate in us! These words of Paul alone would be sufficient to convince us to let Jesus Christ work in us. We see in Jesus Christ and in the church examples of this. God has given us Jesus Christ and the church as signs of his love. Cannot Christ gives us more than we can think? Doesn't the church receive more than it hopes for? God has given us Jesus Christ and the church as signs of his love, yet we still doubt and we still believe that he does not do for us what we desire! O foolishness! It is like a person given one hundred thousand crowns but is worried over five cents. The hundred thousand crowns are to inspire trust in the giver, yet the person hesitates and he defies the giver to give him a cent. They are like animals without reason who prefer a trifle to a treasure.

> I therefore, the prisoner in the Lord, beg you to lead a life worthy of the calling to which you have been called, 2 with all humility and gentleness, with patience, bearing with one another in love, 3 making every effort to maintain the unity of the Spirit in the bond of peace. (Eph 4:1–3)

Paul makes here a short, deductive argument in favor of Christian virtues that maintain true community and hold Christians together. In a community with these virtues, they live with the same dependence and union with one another as members of one body. Paul writes to support them from prison. He prays, and even begs them, to encourage them to live in a way worthy of their calling for the chains that he suffers. My God! These great words! O if the Christian knew his or her calling! He is called to be part of Jesus Christ and to be made one body with him to enjoy his goodness: he is called to become part of God. As it is written, I say, "You are Gods, children of the Most High, all of you" (Ps 82:6), because Jesus Christ has raised up divine grace for people. We do not see God above us but we see God when we participate in the hypostatic union of Jesus Christ. We see this in 2 Peter 1:4 that reads, "Thus he has given us, through these things, his precious and very great promises, so that through them you may escape from the corruption that is in the world because of lust, and may become participants of the divine nature."

Scripture also reads, "What are human beings that you are mindful of them, mortals that you care for them? Yet you have made them a little lower than God, and crowned them with glory and honor?" Psalm 8:4–6. Again we can say that there are people and saints with all the angels in heaven. The vocation of the Christian is to enjoy God and to be consumed with Jesus Christ, "I in them and you in me that they may become completely one" (John 17:23). God calls all Christians to be united in God.

Paul says to live in this grace is a sublime vocation. The virtues of humility and gentleness create peaceful relationships between the faithful. A sweet gentleness comes from humility, yet it is difficult to find a superb person who is gentle. Humility gives us a profound abasement and meekness so that we are not easily tempted into anger. God permits some humiliating situations for a short time so we follow God's great gentleness. When filled with pride, we cannot see God's gentleness. Humility is gentle and gentleness is humble. This is why Jesus Christ does not separate these two virtues. He says, "For I am gentle and humble in heart" (Matt 11:29). Gentleness and humility are absolutely necessary for society because without humility there is no necessary deference and without gentleness there is no respect.

We need to have the support of others, and it is the fruit of charity that we support others. We look at the faithful of the Earth as the most perfect people. We have many natural differences and weaknesses that God annihilates in us. It is good to support even the faults of others with charity, those in our past and those in our future.

But we will not have respect for others long if this is not grounded in our interior. Interior virtue maintains the exterior that is united through the Spirit to God, who unites us to him and to one another. If we are united in God, we all have one Spirit. This unity of the Spirit makes us one in a wonderful peace and we have no more divisions. When we are united with God, we have peace with God and we taste the peace of God. Then we are also united with others, and we have the peace needed to support others. This unity through the Spirit makes us share in the same sentiment and live together in unity.

> There is one body and one Spirit, just as you are called to the one
> hope of your calling 5 one Lord, one faith, one baptism, 6 one God
> and Father of all, who is above all and through all and in all. (Eph
> 4:4–6)

Certainly, all Christians do not now share in one mystical body and because of this, they do not have the same Spirit, that is to say, one shared sentiment. They would be stronger if together they sought redemption. Because they are not one Body, they do not have one Spirit. They lack the

Spirit of the Word. The Spirit of Jesus Christ inspires and infuses us into one Body of Jesus Christ.

But where does one Body and one Spirit come from, when we do not have one hope in God's call to us to have joy in God, when we such different sentiments? Where does one Body and one Spirit come from when there are Christians who even oppose and fight against this joy? It seems we profess a different religion when we see the diversity of sentiments. Sadly, we do not have one Lord and one Faith. We have many conflicts because of heretics and this brings shame to the Christian faith. This is caused by the many differing sentiments that are caused by the fact that we are not in one Spirit and do not have one baptism and one Lord who is the Father of all. God made us to be strong by our unity of Spirit, our sentiments, our heart and our thoughts. Instead, all we have is division! This happens because we leave the will of God. We withdraw from God's unity of Spirit and heart, and simultaneously withdraw from the unity of heart and spirit with our brothers and sisters. Wherever there are souls united to God, they share the same sentiments.

> But each of us was given grace according to the measure of Christ's gift. 8 Therefore it is said,
> "When he ascended on high, he made captivity itself a captive;
> And he gave gifts to men."
> 9 (When it says, "He ascended," what does it mean but that he had also descended into the lower parts of the earth?) (Eph 4:7–9)

All interior people receive a great grace, though everyone receives different degrees of grace. Some receive more than others. But these graces are not, as we imagine, extraordinary gifts, joys, visions and raptures. Instead, the grace of graces that has been given us is Jesus Christ who is over all and gives us this grace. This is what Paul says, *Grace was given to each one of us according to the measure of Christ's gift.*

Paul has shown us that Jesus Christ gives us the gift of grace by comparing two states of spiritual souls. The first state is he *ascended on high, he led a host of captives.* When Jesus Christ wants to end the captivity of stunted souls, what would he do? He takes the soul on high and removes it from what is holding it captive. Jesus Christ leads a host of captives, withdrawing the soul from captivity, and holds the soul close so the soul passes into him.

The second state is that God pours gifts into souls who are destined to live with him. He is pleased to pour large numbers of free gifts and graces into the soul. There is a profound difference between descending and ascending states of being.

These two expressions are found in one person. This is why it pleases our Lord to withdraw the soul from captivity and place our soul in the greatest freedom. When the Lord ends the soul's captivity, the soul moves into a superior place where it openly experiences harsh tests and temptations. Then God sends gifts into the interior part of our human nature and these gifts are a secret power that sustains us. This is what is called the gifts he gave to people.

But in what way does he end the captive's captivity because he goes down to the lowest part, that is to say, in the inferior part of the soul? Jesus Christ brings faith to the captive's nature and wins the soul. He places the soul in the freedom of grace.

Here we are taught the great truth that the measure of height depends on the descent. Jesus Christ descended with power before he was raised up and led the captives out of captivity, that is to say, before he took the nature of the captivity: We must persuade ourselves that before we are raised to happy freedom, we will know a profound abasement and being rejected as the lowest of the Earth.

> He who descended is the same one who ascended far above all the
> heavens, so that he might fill all things. (Eph 4:10)

To confirm what has been said about the raising and the descent, Scripture continues to assure us that *he who descended is raised*. That is to say, the one who is truly annihilated and destroyed is the one who is raised with Jesus Christ who descended to the lowest levels of the earth and is then raised far above all the heavens. The one God destined to the highest heaven first sinks down to the lowest abasement. This power consumes the soul, replenishes it with Christ, and raises the soul to God. Jesus Christ sanctifies the soul that he chooses so that the soul conforms to him. There is no other way for the salvation of the world because Jesus Christ accomplishes and consumes all things by his profound abasement and his following elevation. He does the same to souls through their own descent and then elevation.

> The gifts he gave were that some would be apostles, some prophets,
> some evangelists, some pastors and teachers 12 to equip the saints
> for the work of ministry, for building up the body of Christ, 13
> until all of us come to the unity of the faith and of the knowledge

of the Son of God, to maturity, to the measure of the full stature of
Christ. (Eph 4:11–13)

All the free graces of being an apostle, prophet, evangelist, shepherd
and teacher are given for the building up of the mystical body of Jesus
Christ. God chooses these gifts for his saints and servants.

Jesus Christ uses many different ways in his church, according to the
state of the soul, *until we all attain to the unity of the faith*. Then all the nations are reunited under the same pastor. In John 10:16 Jesus says, "I have
other sheep that do not belong to this fold. I must bring them also, and
they will listen to my voice. So there will be one flock, one shepherd." They
will then all be placed in the spirit of faith that is the true interior spirit. All
humanity is placed in the knowledge of Jesus Christ, and have the same
experiences of Jesus Christ. This experience of the revelation of Jesus Christ
fills the soul with *the measure of the fullness of Christ*. This manifestation of
Jesus Christ brings and fulfills the soul in Christ who deepens chosen souls
abundantly. After all, who can deny that Paul surpasses many other saints?

> We must no longer be children, tossed to and fro about by every
> wind of doctrine, by people's trickery, by their craftiness in deceit-
> ful scheming. 15 But speaking the truth in love, we must grow up
> in every way into him who is the head, into Christ. (Eph 4:14–15)

After the manifestation of Jesus Christ came, we are no longer like
children. When we are children, we have strange hesitations, agitations,
doubts, and perplexities. Unstable, we change frequently. We take one way
in life and then change to another. We do not stay on one path for long.
This perplexing instability comes from our defiance of the true path that
God leads us on. Because of the miseries on God's way, we want to take a
route that appears more certain and more focused on the will of the person.
Yet the soul cannot last long on the self-centered way because withdrawing
from God's way, the soul also withdraws from peace and loses both reason
and reflection. The soul is called to return to God's way. Then the soul is
placed in Jesus Christ in his pure love and truth. The soul believes and is
fulfilled in pure perfection.

> From whom the whole body, joined and knit together by every
> ligament with which it is equipped, as each part is working prop-
> erly, promotes the body's growth in building itself up in love. (Eph
> 4:16)

Jesus Christ transforms and unites the soul with him. As the leader, he sends sweet influences on the soul and quickens the soul. As the leader, he governs and directs everything with an admirable order and in a marvelous way. Then we are not full of hesitations and constant fears caused by reason. Instead, through our abandon Christ influences and governs us. Jesus Christ entirely possesses the soul. That is to say, he gives all the soul's operations dignity merited by his nobility. All the operations of Jesus Christ in the soul are effective operations; all are done in love. All the souls are faithfully reunited in Jesus Christ as the divine leader.

> Now this I affirm and insist on in the Lord: you must no longer live as the Gentiles live, in the futility of their minds. They are darkened in their understanding, alienated from the life of God because of their ignorance and hardness of heart. They have lost all sensibility and have abandoned themselves to licentiousness, greedy to practice every kind of impurity. That is not the way you learned Christ! (Eph 4:17–19)

Here Paul gives a short but forceful description of those people who are not interior. Far from being simple and united under their true leader, they follow multiple instincts and make many mistakes. If they are not interior, they will mistakenly follow vanity.

Paul prays for the interior souls that they remain constant. If they withdraw from being interior and following the way of faith, they will walk in the way of their proper appearance and conduct. They will leave truth behind and become afraid and filled with desires. They then walk in the way of vanity following the error of their own thoughts and reason. If they leave truth behind, their behavior throws them into a profound darkness, like the people of this century, who are not interior but are *full of darkness* and do not know the true light.

In contrast to this, when people follow God's way, they live with abandon and sweetness. If they are raised to the light of God, they will have a life with God. The soul can live with God and not have absurdities, illusions and imaginations. Their heart needs the taste for God so they can taste God's sweetness.

But when they do not live the life of God, this supreme good, they have ignorance in them, due to their hardness of heart. These people do not have either hope or trust in God, but they rely entirely on their own thinking. Instead of trusting God, they rely on propriety. Because of this, they remain wandering around in misery and dissolution.

> That is not the way you learned Christ! For surely you have heard
> about him and were taught in him, as truth is in Jesus. You were
> taught to put away your former way of life, your old self, corrupt
> and deluded by its lusts, and to be renewed in the spirit of your
> minds. (Eph 4:20–23)

After Paul shows all of the errors of those who do not live according to
the interior way, he teaches us the true way of Jesus Christ for those souls
who abandon themselves to him without reserve. These souls surrender
themselves to him after quitting their own conduct. They are taught in him,
as the truth is in Jesus. They listen to what he teaches. Jesus Christ teaches
the soul continually and they do not need to hear anything else. But alas!
How will we be instructed in eternal truth if we never hear it? As David say,
it is necessary to hear it. David says,

> Let me hear what God the Lord will speak,
> for he will speak peace to his people,
> to his faithful, to those who turn to him in their hearts. (Ps 85:8)

Whoever listens to the Lord is perfectly instructed. But, divine Master,
what do you teach the souls who listen to you?

The Lord says it is needed to *put off your old self*, that is, to leave our
former self and all propriety. We leave the first life, which is the life of Adam,
so that we can live the life of Jesus Christ. This first life gives us misleading
and disorderly desires that prevent us from the real truth of Jesus Christ.

But how do we find the way to the real possession of Jesus Christ? It
is very difficult to pretend to have Jesus Christ. Listen to the teachings of
our divine doctor. We must leave the former life so we can enter into the
life of Jesus Christ. We must put off the old self, and if we do not do this,
we cannot receive Jesus Christ. When we leave our former self, we will be
renewed in our interior. Everything happens in our interior. We must leave
the former self behind or all our efforts are in vain.

> And to clothe yourselves with the new self, created according to
> the likeness of God in true righteousness and holiness. So then
> putting away falsehood, let all of us speak the truth to our neigh-
> bors, for we are members of one another. (Eph 4:24–25)

We would not take off the old self if we did not at the same time receive the new self. The old self is made with errors, sins, corruption, and lies
but the new self is made in truth. Jesus Christ gives us the new self that is
created in justice, holiness, and truth.

A soul reborn in the strength of Jesus Christ does not have difficulty speaking with others in truth about Christ. He endured the terrible cross, when the devil provoked rage against him. Christ gained the souls lost by Adam at the beginning of the world. All the persecutions did not stop Christ from speaking the truth, because we are *members one of another* and facing into all other powers, he gained for us the good we have.

> Be angry but do not sin; do not let the sun go down on your anger, 27 and do not make room for the devil. 28 Thieves must give up stealing; rather let them labor and work honestly with their own hands, so as to have something to share with the needy. (Eph 4:26–28)

At times even anger serves the purposes of God and works for the good of the next generation. Some though disobey Paul's counsel and sin by either too much or too little anger. In the first situation, some become angry excessively. By doing this, they sin against God and themselves. They agitate out of bad humor and strangely lose their temper. Rage fills them. To correct them does little good because the principles of self-interest and anger motivate them. They do not have in their heart concern for the glory of God and they look at their brothers only with self-interest. They may violently harm others. Yet if they are superior people, they wait until their anger passes. God does not use these people with such an imperfect principle to correct others.

In the second situation are those who never become angry and hence also displease God. Some anger may serve the purposes of God by working for the good of the next generation. Many good souls abstain from their duty to engage with the next generation and avoid anger by not caring for them. Sadly they bring guilt upon themselves and this needs explaining. We are obligated to take note of the faults of others, and approach them when God asks us to talk to them about their faults. We must not be negligent in our brotherly correction and our duty to them. One reason we do not do our duty rises out of cowardice and fear we will offend God or become angry. Yet God gives us some anger and asks us to talk to them about this fault. Without God we would live quietly in our negligence and timidity. We would never consider the interests of God or the needs of the next generation. Some people speak a just reprimand while feeling angry and believe they have sinned because they lost their temper. Their nature eats away at itself, because they fear that they have offended God, yet this is purely the regret of self-love. These people are right to correct others because they do so with gentleness and sweetness. They need to overlook their small anger (which will happen occasionally) and faithfully continue to guide those under their care.

Therefore, these two types of people have two different ways of conduct. One uses violence to correct others, while the other lacks the proper emotion to correct others. The second can have their fault corrected so they can speak up and the sun will not go down on their anger. They know they have to address evil and correct themselves and their brothers.

I say, the first type when they go into angry rages hurt themselves and create evil. They torment others and bring on themselves humiliation. They become anger; they dwell about the anger, and the anger becomes hatred. Then they do wrong to their neighbor. If no one warns them, these faults will not be corrected by grace. The hatred gives an entrance to the demon in their heart who increases the anger in their heart. Because of this they do not receive their brother into their heart.

Finally Paul says, do not steal, because it is written, *Vengeance is from the Lord.* If we steal from someone, we harm him or her. Instead, we should use the authority the Lord has put in our hands. We are to use all our powers to nourish the poor in the material sense. Also, we pour succor on poor souls with the richness of his grace and when they are in need, we help them.

> Let no evil talk come out of your mouths, but only such as is good
> for building up, as there is need, so that your words may give grace
> to those who hear. (Eph 4:29)

This wisdom is necessary for the virtues of Christians because nothing is more pernicious than malicious conversation. However, it is true that a heart living with God does not engage in evil talk. Our Savior says, "For out of the abundance of the heart the mouth speaks" Matthew 12:34. In other words, the mouth is the expression of the heart. Some discourse is innocent in appearance but actually indifferent to the needs of their neighbor. When we are with God, it becomes difficult for us to speak of other things. We want only to speak of things that edify their neighbors. To help the neighbor, we should talk with simplicity, candor and happiness. This discourse offers both instruction and help.

Paul says that when we speak to others about faith, this interior faith grounds and perfects the exterior. But, O, grand partisan of the faith, how do you speak of this faith to those who may take the word of faith for a word of scandal? However, this word of faith has the advantage of giving grace to those who listen. We receive eternity by listening. For those who have ears to hear, grace is communicated to them.

> And do not grieve the Holy Spirit of God, with which you were marked with a seal for the day of redemption. (Eph 4:30)

Jesus Christ died for us so he could be in our heart and so that we are animated through him. Therefore, through the Spirit we have the seal for the day of redemption. When we are contrite, the Holy Spirit prevents sins from coming in. Yet we grieve the Holy Spirit of God when we do not receive faith in our hearts and dwell with God in our interior. If we refuse the Holy Spirit and say it is scandalous, we grieve the Holy Spirit.

> Put away from you all bitterness and wrath and anger and wrangling and slander, together with all malice, and be kind to one another, tenderhearted, forgiving one another, as God in Christ has forgiven you. (Eph 4:31–32)

Here Paul corrects the faults that are interior. It is the interior that gives the sweetness of the Spirit and the support for others. When we are interior, we have tolerance in the face of insults and forgive easily. We do not wish evil for our neighbor. It is the faithful interior that banishes from the heart all malice.

> Therefore be imitators of God, as beloved children, and live in love, as Christ loved us and gave himself for us, a fragrant offering and sacrifice to God. (Eph 5:1–2)

If Jesus Christ tells us, "Be perfect, therefore, as your heavenly Father is perfect" (Matt 5:48) and Paul tell us *to imitate God*, we must not look upon this as something impossible. How do we imitate God? By sharing God's simplicity and love. Jesus Christ says that his Sun shines on the just and the sinners: in the same way we must show beneficence and goodness to the just and the unjust, to those who do good and to those who do evil.

Brotherly love and support of the neighbor is both necessary and difficult. It is necessary because without love it is impossible to please God. We also need love to have a conversation with another person, or even to live in society. It is difficult because of our differences in our moods and temperaments. We need to be strongly grounded in goodness so we can love our neighbors with their faults and foibles. We must have a sweet and tender love for our brothers *to imitate Jesus Christ*, who offered himself in sacrifice and lives in God for us, a sacrificial victim for our expiation. He carries our pains and burdens for us. It is for us that he was sacrificed. There are some souls that are also sacrificed and bear the impurity and propriety of others.

> But fornication and impurity of any kind, or greed, must not even
> be mentioned among you, as is proper among saints. Entirely out
> of place is obscene, silly, and vulgar talk; but instead, let there be
> thanksgiving. (Eph 5:3–4)

This wisdom is extremely important for Christians. We cannot accept the discourse of impurity under any pretext because then we walk by the light of impurity. Yet only a few people humbly speak out to stop these temptations of impurity. It is very necessary to speak out against impurity. Through this we banish temptation and God gives us many graces.

Some say untrue things under the pretext of trust or friendship. This secret light of fire appears like a small thing in the beginning, almost like nothing. But if we engage in this pretense, it lights a blaze that quickly spreads and destroys things in strange ways.

The *words of mockery and buffoonery* are not worthy for Christians. They must be absolutely banished from those who serve God. This is an important discipline that they must struggle against with all their might and without which they will never have an interior life. These words are not worthy of the vocation of a Christian. For these distracting words are only directed to human glory, pleasure and entertainment.

> Be sure of this, that no fornicator or impure person, or one who
> is greedy (that is, an idolater), has any inheritance in the kingdom
> of Christ and of God. Let no one deceive you with empty words,
> for because of these things the wrath of God comes on those who
> are disobedient. Therefore do not be associated with them. (Eph
> 5:5–7)

These sins are those that are entirely opposed to the reign of Jesus Christ and the love of God because impurity brings the idolatry of human pleasure that is preferred over God. Avarice makes us a slave to money. These two passions will fill the human heart and control it continually. Then there is no resting place for God within the heart and there is no yielding to Jesus Christ. If we let these two passions lead us, then we obey them without resistance. They corrupt the heart, and they leave no entry for grace. It is rare that when a miser is converted that he or she looks upon greed as a sin, but instead calls it by the name of justice.

The worst evil that can happen to young people is to engage in the vanity of dissolute beliefs or libertarianism. If they have gone far into folly and extravagance in their thinking, then they doubt the mysteries of religion and finally they doubt God himself. With all their horrible distractions, they believe that all their sins are permitted because they doubt all things, and they believe in the gallantry of fights. Finally, they openly commit all sins. They believe that the immortality of the soul is a fairy tale. They have become insensible to everything that is said to them and become hardened to grace. By this, they attract the anger of God to them. We must avoid having interactions with them more than we do death and hell.

> For once you were darkness, but now in the Lord you are light. Live as children of light—for the fruit of the light is found in all that is good and right and true. Try to find out what is pleasing to the Lord. Take no part in the unfruitful works of darkness, but instead expose them. (Eph 5:8–11)

At the beginning of the Letter to the Ephesians, Paul says that what is most spiritual and interior is the manifestation of Jesus Christ. Now he shows us how to get there. He tells us in detail both the things we must do and the things we must avoid to reach the interior life. His counsels are both just and proper. Paul leaves nothing out. To begin, we must first embrace the faith in a conversion for *once we were in darkness* but now we are in the light. Now we renounce the errors and distractions of darkness to enter into the true light of the interior. In this light, we walk and live.

We bear fruit for eternity. That is, he says, all that is good and right and true. In the duty we have the obligation to do good full of mercy and sweetness.

Paul shows us the development of our works. The soul, after having exercised goodness, even with a small power, is placed in the state in the first degree to exercise justice. The exercise of that justice reaches to God, to the neighbor, and to our own self. Reaching to God, to whom we attribute all things, we look for everything in Him and nothing outside of Him. Reaching to our neighbor, we keep the perfect rules of charity; we love the neighbor as we love ourselves. When we look at God, we see ourselves as full of nothingness and sin. The soul is in a perfect state of justice when it is placed in truth. Then she knows that exercising justice is not a virtue, but truth. The soul by sight, thought or feeling, understands truth, and sees other things also that are in truth.

But before the soul arrives there (through the graces of the pure goodness of God), we must seek and do the will of God in all things in order to please Him, to avoid all that displeases him and to condemn all that he condemns.

> But everything exposed by the light becomes visible, for everything that becomes visible is light. Therefore it says,
>
> "Sleeper, awake!
> Rise from the dead,
> And Christ will shine on you." (Eph 5:13–14)

There are two awakenings to awaken from the sleep of death. The first awakening is to awaken from our sins to enter into the grace of Jesus Christ. Jesus Christ must shine light on us with the light of his grace and he does this. But how does he shine light on us? First, he takes us to an interior place and shows us our ingratitude and the disorders of our life. This gives us pain and horror but it is the proper light to awaken us from the first death.

The other awakening happens when we *rise from the dead*. This is for mystical and interior souls who come to the end of their miseries in the darkness of the mystical death, who contemplate, and *awaken from their sleep, rise from the dead, and Christ will shine on them*. This happens only by the light of his grace, because they had never had more grace than when they were in this most profound darkness. This happens through Jesus Christ himself. O, then they are surprised that the light of Jesus Christ holds on to all of us, in life and time and light.

The difference from the first enlightenment is that they are illumined by Jesus Christ himself, and in him is their light, as it is written in the Revelation 21: 23, "And the city has no need of sun or moon to shine on it, for the glory of God is its light, and its lamp is the Lamb." The sun and moon were created by grace, but as the Scripture says, *the Lamb himself will be your light.* Therefore, the Lamb and God will be their light. Also, it says that light captures us and makes us see that all that is discovered is light. For example, we do not discover sins and accusations through darkness but we discover the way through light. We discover Jesus Christ himself. We discover the way of nothingness and misery through light and not darkness. We do not look at things but we look at the truth, and while gazing at truth, we are purified by this same truth that enlightens us.

> Be careful then how you live, not as unwise people but as wise, making the most of the time, because the days are evil. So do

not be foolish, but understand what the will of the Lord is. (Eph 5:15–17)

The wisdom that Paul speaks about is not the wisdom of the flesh because he condemns that in several places. But the wisdom that Paul desires is that which makes us defy ourselves so that we abandon ourselves to God. The act of folly is when one is weak and relies on an imaginary strength to fight against powerful enemies. True wisdom sees our own weakness against powerful enemies yet gives us power so we may overcome them.

This is the wisdom that Paul asks of us. Following this, he writes saying to redeem the time, because the days are evil. We can only have this redemption of our time and our ordeals with a complete abandonment to God. Unless we abandon ourselves to God, our days are long and evil. The more we abandon, the days diminish their evil and are not as hard and rough. Therefore he says again, "Do not be foolish, but understand what the will of the Lord is." True wisdom is the knowledge of the will of God without reservation. Our Lord Jesus Christ says once in his gospel to *be wise* and he compares us with the *serpent*. Matthew 10:16 reads, "So be wise as serpents and innocent as doves." This shows us what wisdom he asks of us. The serpent has two wisdoms. First, he uses his body to protect his head. In the same way, we must lose everything to protect our master Jesus Christ. The second wisdom is that he leaves his old skin to take the new. In the same way, we must leave the old human to put on the new.

> Do not get drunk with wine, for that is debauchery, but be filled with the Spirit, as you sing psalms and hymns and spiritual songs among yourselves, singing and making melody to the Lord in your hearts. (Eph 5: 18–19)

Nothing is as sweet and agreeable as the way that Paul asks. Nothing is sweeter than chanting the Psalms with such an innocent pleasure. Interior souls are given understanding of what the Psalms contain, in which they find an inconceivable sweet suavity and sensitive pleasure. In times of affliction, nothing has more consolation than to chant the Psalms written by the afflicted David. In times of joy, there are Psalms that fill you with delight. You find in the Psalms all moods, but to taste the pleasures of the Psalms, you must be interior.

Paul warns of the excess of wine. It is certain that too much wine and food is extremely opposed to the freedom of the Spirit and is incompatible with the interior. You must be sober to be able to receive the impressions of grace. If you hope to have a rich and full justice, it must be of the Holy Spirit.

> Giving thanks to God the Father at all times and for everything in the name of our Lord Jesus Christ. 21 Be subject to one another out of reverence for Christ. (Eph 5:20–21)

Always give thanks to God for both the good and evil. When we see that God has all things, we do not attribute any evil to the creature but we look upon everything as coming from God. The things that God allows are for our greatest good. In this strength we give thanks to God for our Lord Jesus Christ. Then we submit easily to others because of God's order in which we are placed. We do not look at the human order, but we look to God. It is to God only that we submit ourselves.

> Wives, be subject to your husbands as you are to the Lord. For the husband is the head of the wife just as Christ is the head of the church, the body of which he is the Savior. Just as the church is subject to Christ, so also wives ought to be, in everything to their husbands. Husbands, love your wives, just as Christ loved the church and gave himself up for her, in order to make her holy by cleansing her with the washing of water by the word, so as to present the church to himself in splendor, without a spot or wrinkle or anything of the kind—yes, so that she may be holy and without blemish. In the same way, husbands should love their wives as they do their own bodies. He who loves his wife loves himself. For no one ever hates his own body, but he nourishes and tenderly cares for it, just as Christ does for the church, because we are members of his body. For this reason a man will leave his father and mother and be joined to his wife, and the two will become one flesh. This is a great mystery, and I am applying it to Christ and the church. Each of you, however, should love his wife as himself, and a wife should respect her husband. (Eph 5:22–32)

Women should be devoted to their husbands and families, but libertine women do not do this. These women become like harpies and do not serve their families. Without a good attachment to their family, wives can end up despising their families and in financial ruin with excessive debt. Some excessively spiritual women also do this. They do not care for their husbands. They do not want to practice the virtues. All they want is to leave the cares of their husbands and family and run from church to church, confessor to confessor, to avoid yielding to the husband and family. While the woman is at church, the children are corrupted and the servants are distracted with nonsense. These women seek only to please and entertain themselves and will never be satisfied.

The true devotion of a married woman is to live the life of a married woman. Wives should want to please their husbands and their families. To find fulfillment, they must have a true devotion to their families and not speak excessive rebukes to anyone.

I have put these words of Paul's together because they are about a single subject, which is about the church of God. I think all the evils and disorders come because we do not know enough about the holy and the profane. Problems in marriage cause problems in the church. In marriage are born all the disorders that finally arrive in the church of God. We do not respect the glorious grace of marriage that is designed for the glory of God and the public good. I think that today marriage serves as a cover for all sorts of crimes. Marriage is not then a divine union between a man and a woman but it is a narrow liaison made of blood and nature. We must leave our natural father and mother if we are to receive the gift of marriage.

But where this disunion come from? It is when people do not follow the wisdom of Paul. Respect and deference must be mutual between husbands and wives. If we follow this advice of Paul, all the church of God will be reformed because mothers and fathers are united. They would raise their children in harmony and in the fear of God. The children would see the glories of the Christian life. Instead, children witness the deformity and corruption of their parents' conflicts before the children can even reason.

What is the source of these troubles? First, we bring no faith to the marriage and it becomes full of crimes. I have said, and will say again, I wish with all my heart, those married should exercise their duties toward their families and find sanctification in this way. Secondly, arranged marriages should not take place because the couple might have no sympathy of feelings and their lives are then filled with trouble. Thirdly, we must also let those who want religious vocations and wish to work in the church take their religious vows instead of marriage. No one should be forced into marriage.

Marriages should be holy as it is instituted by Jesus Christ for the world. Yet today many desecrate marriage.

> Children, obey your parents in the Lord, for this is right. "Honor your father and mother"—this is the first commandment with a promise: "so that it may be well with you and you may live long on the earth." (Eph 6:1–3)

Obedience to the father and the mother is both natural and divine law. If we disobey this law, we disobey all the laws. Yet frequently the bad example of arguing parents makes children disobedient. The lack of respect between the mother and father causes rebellion also in the children. The children lose their fear of parents and of God.

As these problems become worse, the parents become more unreasonable. Or they might accept many forms of bad conduct in the children without correcting them.

However, some children become corrupt, even with the parents' best efforts and good education. The parents do everything they can to help the child, yet nothing works. The children rebel against those who have given them life. But these children make bad mistakes in their lives because of their ingratitude.

Yet God listens to the prayers, sacrifices and sufferings of the parents and sees the impiety of the children. This is why fathers and mothers must pray for the conversion of their children and imitate Monica, the mother of St. Augustine. The parents must always sacrifice and continue to pray for their children. This is the best way to obtain results from their prayers.

> Fathers, do not provoke your children to anger, but bring them up
> in the discipline and instruction of the Lord. (Eph 5:4)

Certainly many fathers and mothers treat their children with great injustice. They treat some of their children with favoritism and cause jealousy among the children. When parents prefer some children, the other children are reduced to being slaves and scapegoats of the favored ones. The mother and father despise and abuse these rejected children. If the mothers and fathers are violent, they frequently hit and hurt children. This changes the children's natural sweet disposition into an angry and ferocious one.

> Slaves, obey your earthly masters with fear and trembling, in
> singleness of heart, as you obey Christ; 6 not only while being
> watched, and in order to please them, but as slaves of Christ, doing
> the will of God from the heart. 7 Render service with enthusiasm,
> as to the Lord and not to men and women, 8 knowing that what-
> ever good we do, we will receive the same again from the Lord,
> whether we are slaves or free. (Eph 6:5–8)

If we follow this wisdom of Paul, wonderful peace will reign in our lives. Slaves serve well out of fear, but where is the simplicity and surrender? They revolt against their masters and when the master is gone, they plunder and steal the belongings. Or if they serve, they do not regard God in this service with respect and affection. If they love God, they support their corrections. But where do we find such slaves? If the masters are sweet and affable, the slaves might not be.

> And, masters, do the same to them. Stop threatening them, for you know that both of you have the same Master in heaven, and with him there is no partiality. (Eph 6:9)

If slaves must have respect, submission, and obedience to the masters, the masters must show charity and support to the slaves. They must not be violent to the slaves and use kindness instead of force. They must stop all anger, injuries and bad treatment. Because slaves are the slaves of Jesus Christ, they must be regarded as human beings. You serve the same God. You must correct any faults with charity.

If we follow all of Paul's wisdom, we would not need to seek outside counsel for the conduct of families, politics, and for the good order of the government. Instead, we would look to God within our interior life.

> Finally, be strong in the Lord and in the strength of his power. 11
> Put on the whole armor of God, so that you may be able to stand against the wiles of the devil. (Eph 6:10–11)

Paul not only educates us about the good we must do and the evil we must avoid. He gives us armor to defend ourselves from the enemies that oppose and conquer us. But what armor does he give? Does he tell us to use all our own strength? Our strength alone does not defend us because our self-interested hearts are weak with corruption.

But what does Paul tell us? Be strong in the Lord, which means to be strong in the power that is all-powerful. In this strength, we receive the armor of God. We are united with God in all pain, temptations and attacks. Our weakness will receive his strength. Our powerlessness will receive his power. Our misery will receive his virtue. It is impossible for us to defend ourselves against all the schemes of the Devil. How can we defend ourselves when we do not know what the schemes are and the illusions appear to us as truth? We must abandon ourselves to God and remain in his hands in all situations. He will defend us himself, according to this beautiful passage: "Commit your way to the Lord; trust in him, and he will act" (Ps 37: 5). And also, "The Lord will fight for you, and you have only to keep still" (Exod 14:14). But, we say, if I become idle, then the devil attacks and surprises me easily. No, the point is not to become idle, for we are active.

We abandon ourselves in his arms and give ourselves to God to fight for us. There we remain in security trusting yourself to his strength. It is an impenetrable citadel where the devil has no advantage over us. Jesus Christ opened his arms and his heart for us to receive this, and we are hidden from our enemies.

> For our struggle is not against enemies of flesh and blood, but against the rulers, against the authorities, against the cosmic powers of this present darkness, against the spiritual forces of evil in the heavenly places. (Eph 6:12–13)

Our strength is nothing. If we fight with our own insights, we will be conquered. Because our enemies are powerful, we do not have enough strength to defeat them.

We do, though, have the weapon of the invincible armor of God. This armor fights all of our battles in this life with good consequences, whether they are against the world, flesh, and demons. The armor of the Lord fights against our own hypocrisy and propriety. Through the armor of God, Jesus Christ will conquer our enemies.

> Stand therefore, and fasten the belt of truth around your waist, and put on the breastplate of righteousness. 15 As shoes for your feet put on whatever will make you ready to proclaim the gospel of peace. 16 With all of these, take the shield of faith, with which you will be able to quench all the flaming arrows of the evil one. (Eph 6:14–16)

"Stand therefore" means to continue in grace through our union with God. Our connection with God makes us strong. Truth must surround the soul to keep out any lie. For the belt of truth is as much interior as exterior. In interior truth we are annihilated by the grandeur of God, and we are placed in righteousness and simplicity. Exterior truth means our words are the same as the ones we think and our actions are without guile.

Jesus Christ clothes us with the *breastplate of righteousness*. This is a justice that is not self-centered and proprietary. God gives this justice and we receive it without violence. Christ clothes us with justice, protecting our interior life.

God gives us *shoes for our feet* that carry us out to love God with purity and to do his will. Strong souls *proclaim the gospel of peace*, while being renewed. When the gospel converts, our sensuality is converted. Then we know *the gospel of interior peace*, an experience that astonishes and surprises us.

That is why Paul recommends that *faith* serve as a *shield*. The shield repels blows and strikes. The devil can do nothing to a faithful soul. Faith and confidence in God place us in security, so that if the Devil attacks, his arrows only turn against him. God himself fights for us as he did for Abraham, who offered sacrifices showing his faith. We never need to fear the devil.

> Take the helmet of salvation, and the sword of the Spirit, which is the word of God. (Eph 6:17)

Hope supports the soul. When filled with hope, we are emptied of concerns, thoughts, and worries. Hope is the guardian of the Spirit and keeps our imagination emptied of falsities and phantoms. When we hope, the devil is not able to attack us. Hope becomes like a helmet that tempers any ordeal. The Spirit becomes like a sword. The sword protects the church of Jesus Christ from its enemies. This sword is the Word of God.

> Pray in the Spirit at all times, in every prayer and supplication. To that end keep alert and always persevere in supplication for all the saints. (Eph 6:18)

Paul says that we must in all times and at all places pray in the interior to God. If we do not pray in the Spirit, there are wars of faith without hope, truth or justice.

This prayer is by Christ and not by ourselves. O the wonderful way that God shows his favor for us! But how does he do this? When we abandon ourselves to him without reserve, only thinking of him, he sees and thinks continually of us. Paul says we are to pray for others according to the will and movement of God. All prayers in the will of God are for us and the benefit of the faithful. All prayers are in Jesus Christ according to his merits.

> Pray also for me, so that when I speak, a message may be given to me to make known with boldness the mystery of the gospel, 20 for which I am an ambassador in chains. Pray that I may declare it boldly, as I must speak . . . 23 Peace be to the whole community, and love with faith, from God the Father and the Lord Jesus Christ. 24 Grace be with all who have an undying love for our Lord Jesus Christ. (Eph 6:19–20, 23–24)

How can Paul preach in chains and be an ambassador of the Gospel in a dungeon? This is the secret of the apostolic state and a soul that has arrived in God. He both speaks and preaches in God. His prayers have conquered his words. Paul in prison and chains is the conquest of Jesus Christ, as Jesus Christ has conquered on the cross. O happy chains, you are fruitful and you are never sterile! Paul wrote this epistle that God gave him in prison so that through all the centuries, we would be instructed by it.

Finally, Paul ends this Epistle by wishing faith, love, and peace for us. The person who has faith and love, also has peace. Paul desires that *grace be unto all who have an undying love for Jesus Christ*. This grace of graces and the source of all graces is Christ's pure love: without it all the other graces are not graces. God gives purity and pure love.

Guyon's *Commentary on Paul's Letter to the Colossians with Explanations and Reflections on the Interior Life*

> For this reason since the day we heard it, we have not ceased praying for you and asking that you may be filled with the knowledge of God's will in all spiritual wisdom and understanding, 10 so that you may lead lives worthy of the Lord, fully pleasing to him, as you bear fruit in every good work and as you grow in the knowledge of God. (Col 1:9–10)

PAUL SAYS THAT TO lead lives worthy of the Lord, we must know the will of God. Works that appear impressive are nothing if they are not the will of God. This is why Paul asks us to be *filled with the knowledge of God's will.* The gift of knowing God's will is the gift of all wisdom, science, and intelligence. In fact, the will of God gives all intelligence and science. Perfection of life is accomplished only through intelligence given through this will.

Nothing is accomplished without the will of God. When living in the will of God, we please God and bear fruit in these works. Because the soul knows God, the soul accomplishes God's will.

> May you be made strong with all the strength that comes from his glorious power, and may you be prepared to endure everything with patience, while joyfully 12 giving thanks to the Father, who has enabled you to share in the inheritance of the saints in light. (Col 1:11–12)

To accomplish the will of God in all things means that the soul is made strong with a majestic power and nothing shakes her. The self does not have this power in herself but the will of God communicates this generous and unlimited power to the believer. The soul then has no weakness but experiences great calm. The soul suffers with joy and does not grow weary, even under extreme afflictions.

This is true, my God! Your yoke is easy and your burden light (Matt 11:30)! Although it seems that the weight of immense afflictions will overwhelm the soul, yet you support her with divine power so that she can carry any heavy weight and load. You give the grace of light to know and accomplish your will, so that the soul shares in the inheritance of the saints. This participation in the will brings suffering that blesses and sanctifies. The faithful share in the cross and suffering.

> He has rescued us from the power of darkness and transferred us into the kingdom of his beloved Son, 14 in whom we have redemption, the forgiveness of sin. (Col 1:13–14)

God rescued us from the power of darkness by the power of his will. We know that Adam disobeyed the will of God so he could follow his own will and thus subjected humanity to the power of darkness. Because Jesus Christ followed the will of his Father, humanity could leave the power of darkness and obey the will of God. The Son's obedience to grace allows us to obey the will of God. Because of this, the light of God reveals his will to us and through faith allows us to practice it. This removes us from the power of darkness and transfers us into the kingdom of his beloved Son.

What is the kingdom of his Son? The kingdom of God is within the Father. We enter the kingdom through the blood of Jesus Christ when we follow the will of God. Jesus Christ reigns in us and welcomes our participation in the Kingdom. Jesus Christ has accomplished all of this for us through the sacrifice of his blood. The blood of Jesus Christ merits this grace for us and cleanses us of our sins.

> He is the image of the invisible God, the firstborn of all creation; 16 for in him all things in heaven and on earth were created, things visible and invisible, whether thrones or dominions or rulers or powers—all things have been created through him and for him. (Col 1:15–16)

The eternal decree of the Father created everything in Christ who is the eternal image of God the Father, the firstborn of all creation. For in

Christ everything was made on heaven and earth, and nothing was made that was not for him. All creatures were created in Jesus Christ and were created for him.

The infallible will of God through Jesus Christ has created humanity. The world and all creatures, both heavenly and terrestrial, have all been created in Jesus Christ by his Word and for his Word. Christ produces the eternal, begotten Word in human beings made in his image and forms the eternal image of the Son in their interior. All the strength that humans have is contained in God. The Word expresses himself in humans and places them in eternity. God desires immortality for human beings. The moment they were created, God took pleasure in expressing and imprinting the image of the Word in them. This desire of God existed before they were created. Humanity lived in God's will before the Fall, yet the Fall damaged the image of God in human beings. Now human beings may live eternally in the will of God and in the eternal decree of the Son. This is why when we have chosen God, we are absorbed into Him and strong in Him.

> He himself is before all things, and in him all things hold together. (Col 1:17)

God is before all and all is in him. There are no things, not only real but even possible, that are not contained in God. Creatures cannot exist without him, because they exist only in and through him. Living creatures of both heaven and earth are created by him and preserved by the Word. It is by him they are made. All creatures come from God because all have been made by his wisdom.

> He is the head of the body, the church; he is the beginning, the firstborn from the dead, so that he might come to have first place in everything. (Col 1:18)

Jesus Christ as the Word is the principle and essence of life for all who live. All life emanates from him. Jesus as both God and man is the head of the church and gives us his life.

Paul says that Christ is the firstborn from the dead. But how is he the firstborn from the dead? He does this in two ways. As both God and human, Christ always lived in God and knew no death through sin. His life gives life to all those who are dead through sin. The second way is his resurrection from the tomb because of God's power and strength. He is the first resurrected from the dead. Because of his resurrection, we are all resurrected.

Christ is the animating power of all things, as he answers the woman at the well, "I am he, the one who is speaking to you" (John 4:26). He is the destined first, the first of the faithful, the first in resurrection and the first without participation in death. But why is he the principle in all things? It is because:

For in him all the fullness of God was pleased to dwell. (Col 1:19)

All the fullness of God lives in Jesus Christ. God the Father pours himself constantly into Jesus Christ, communicating to Jesus all the fullness that he is. Jesus communicates to us all that God the Father communicates to him. The Father and the Son and the Holy Spirit share their life-giving love with us. This communication has no sin because the fullness of God resides in the Trinity. The Father flows entirely into the Son and fills the Son with the fullness of his being. The Son returns this same fullness of being to the Father. The Holy Spirit fully communicates with the Father and the Son.

While in this world, Jesus Christ had all the fullness of being of God and he communicated this to people. This is why he is always the living principle who communicates life without sin to people. He receives everything in him. He is the beginning and the end in all things, as it says in the Apocalypse. "'I am the Alpha and the Omega,' says the Lord God, who is and who was and who is to come, the Almighty" (Rev 1:8).

And through him God was pleased to reconcile to himself all things, whether on earth or in heaven, by making peace through the blood of his cross. (Col 1:20)

God has reconciled all things to himself through Jesus Christ. Because of sin, things were divided apart that had formerly been one. God's essence is love; sin divides us from God's love. Sin divides us from God and each other. As an example, we see in Mark 9: 14–29 how the spirit of the demon and sin disunites people from God and from other people. Hell separates people from God. Christ came to end this separation and reconcile humanity with God.

Christ's Spirit unites all things in union with God. Jesus Christ reconciles us to his Father, and the Father by this reconciliation receives us. As it is said, we are transferred to the Kingdom of the Son by his love. The love of the Son supports us in his Kingdom with the love of the Father. We love by him, in him, and for him.

Jesus Christ by the effusion of his blood has reconciled us eternally with the Father and we are reunited in the love from which we were separated. He makes a double reconciliation in all that is on heaven and on earth. He reconciles the charity and love of God with the charity and love of human beings and ends all division of human being with human being and all humanity with God. He brings peace with his blood to both heaven and earth.

> And you who were once estranged and hostile in mind, doing evil deeds, 22 he has now reconciled in his fleshly body through death, so as to present you holy and blameless and irreproachable before him—23 provided that you continue securely established and steadfast in the faith, without shifting from the hope promised by the gospel that you heard, which has been proclaimed to every creature under heaven. I, Paul, became a servant of this gospel. (Col 1:21–23)

While in sin and estranged from God, we follow chaos. Before conversion, we are deprived of grace and true love. Living as enemies of God, we do evil deeds. Without Jesus Christ, we would remain eternally an enemy of God.

Jesus is truth. We need to approach Jesus Christ who reconciles us with his Father. He gives us grace to remove the desire to commit iniquities and in its place he gives us virtues of love and understanding. In this first reconciliation, Jesus Christ's death brings us grace for virtues.

Believers, though, can have struggles. In Romans 7:15, Paul says, "I do not understand my own actions. For I do not do what I want, but I do the very thing I hate." The faithful person here is not an enemy of God but still has disorders like she did before conversion. She wants to love and be with Jesus Christ. In this state God changes her from being an enemy by destroying the cruel tyrant of self-adulation within the soul; this self-adulation is an irreconcilable enemy. Therefore after destroying and tearing out the idol of self-worship, God declares she is not an enemy and she loves God even more because of his mercy. Her heart now gives a profound testimony to God.

Now the soul faces a great challenge. The conversion left the soul without power or strength to fight or the ability to defend herself. The soul must repose in God without strength or power. The soul has spent all its power in the first combat against self-love when converted. Yet now after conversion, waves of power and challenge begin to hit her. Like a drowning person, she loses all strength in fighting the water, so now the soul must be carried by the waves, without making new efforts, because all strength has been spent.

She feels the waves might prevail and she might perish without power or strength to fight or the ability to defend herself. She has no health in the natural; the waves show her no strength and no pity. The waves become increasingly ruthless and cruel. She is surrounded on all sides and no one comes to help. No creature gives her a hand. She no longer hopes for human assistance. She prays to heaven because nothing in life seems solid. She hears no voice. The waves suffocate her. She awaits death.

What is happening here? This grace of Jesus Christ, after having drawn the soul out of the belly of sin, then exposes the soul to waves, just like Moses to the waves and tempests on the Red Sea, just like Jesus Christ was also exposed to the waves in Matthew 8:24 "A windstorm arose on the sea, so great that the boat was being swamped by the waves; but he was asleep." Then the soul says like Job 7:8, "The eye that beholds me will see me no more; while your eyes are upon me, I shall be gone."

This is then the second death accomplished by the operation of grace through the death of Jesus Christ. This is that which makes the *new reconciliation*. This is when the human finds her health in perishing. She is like Job who says, "I have no hope" (Job 13:15). Yet the unfaithful and unpitying waves, against which she has fought a long time, become a sea through which the grace of Jesus Christ is communicated, giving the soul a new life. When she hopes no longer and sees only death, then a door opens and carries her into a harbor, where she is revived. When she believed she was about to suffocate and die, then Christ gives new life.

The grace of the death of Jesus Christ makes the soul pure and holy before him.

But what has Paul said here? This happens, he says, to those who remain securely established and steadfast in the faith, without shifting away from hope. I think we must hope even in despair and believe even while perishing. Life seems contrary to us. New life happens when we do not hope in our own strength and no one comes to our rescue. Then we must believe and hope in the all-powerful divine. At no point do we hope in ourselves, but we hope in God.

I must explain this. In our loss we find our salvation by hoping only in God. We hope to serve God's righteousness and interests and we will perish for him. All is for God's glory and honor in our death. Job is very clear. When he was at the end and in the most extreme desolation, hope replenished in his bosom, and he believed that his Redeemer was alive. Job says, "For I know that my Redeemer lives" (Job 19:25). This is essential life.

All the death that I feel cannot change God's power. I know that he lives and that he is my Redeemer. He can save me. I want no other salvation than that which he gives. My Redeemer lives, and that's enough. Therefore, I hope that I will see "the goodness of the Lord in the land of the living" (Ps 27:13) and that my death will give me more knowledge of his life.

> I am now rejoicing in my sufferings for your sake, and in my flesh
> I am completing what is lacking in Christ's afflictions for the sake
> of his body, that is, the church. (Col 1:24)

Jesus Christ completed his passion and all he had to suffer. He was entirely consumed. Through his suffering, Jesus Christ was consummated. But Jesus Christ wants to extend and offer his passion and suffering into the church and its members. This is the goal of life: to imitate and express Jesus Christ. As Paul has said this, I will not repeat it here, except to say this. All the states of Jesus Christ are still expressed in the world both in general and in particular ways. When they have been fully expressed, the world will end. Therefore, Paul has had to complete, according to this passage, what is lacking in Christ's afflictions for the sake of his body, the church. That is to say, Jesus Christ extends his passion in each member of the church who participates in his body. Paul along with other faithful complete what was lacking in the afflictions of Jesus Christ.

> I became its servant according to God's commission that was given
> to me for you, to make the Word of God fully known, 26 the mys-
> tery that has been hidden throughout the ages and generations
> but has now been revealed to his saints. 27 To them God chose to
> make known how great among the Gentiles are the riches of this
> mystery, which is Christ in you, the hope of glory. (Col 1:25–27)

Jesus Christ was hidden from all the people of the ancient law. Some holy prophets had discovered and proven this presence of the Word of God within them, but most people ignored these things. Jesus Christ was not content only to live on earth for thirty-three years among people but his divinity lives in all humanity in a very special and particular way. The church testifies to the richness of his mystery and grace, which is Christ in us, the hope of glory. Finally, I say, Christ came to announce this in his Gospel, and he wants this preached throughout the world.

This Gospel tells us the truth of the wonderful mystery, that is, Christ came to live within us. This Gospel that Jesus Christ lives within us, though, is almost ignored throughout the world. Jesus Christ does not only want this to be preached, but he chose the communion for us to see the possibility and truth of this. We need to comprehend the truth of his living within us and to be assured by this.

Paul has chosen in a particular way to preach this wonderful gospel about the home of God within us. No other apostle writes in such a particular way about the interior faith as Paul does.

This is the mystery that Jesus Christ wants to presently reveal and will be discovered within his church.

> It is he whom we proclaim, warning everyone and teaching everyone in all wisdom, so that we may present everyone mature in Christ. 29 For this I toil and struggle with all the energy that he powerfully inspires within me. (Col 1:28–29)

Paul says that we are to proclaim the mystery of the presence of God and our home in Jesus Christ. Because of Christ, we can have true perfection through the true perfection of God. It is impossible to have this perfection in any other way except the interior. It is the interior faith that we must preach throughout the world. As Paul says, the power of God's grace attracts others to Christ.

It is a strange thing that these fundamental principles of the Christian religion preached by Jesus Christ and by the apostles must today be fought against. They choose imperfection over perfection and cry out against true perfection as if it is dangerous and to be feared.

> For I want you to know how much I am struggling for you, and for those in Laodicea, and for all who have not seen me face to face. 2 I want their hearts to be encouraged and united in love, so that they may have all the riches of assured understanding and have the knowledge of God's mercy, that is, Christ himself, 3 in whom are hidden all the treasures of wisdom and knowledge. (Col 2:1–3)

There are two types of intelligence. In the first intelligence, reason seems to control wisdom. Reason struggles a long time and sometimes seems to prevail over wisdom. This is an unstable intelligence that vacillates and changes because of this struggle between wisdom and reason. We believe that reason is truth because its light seems to be full of intelligence. But this is mistaken and the deception is soon discovered. For wisdom suddenly expresses itself and truth is seen. To give the soul perfect intelligence, it is necessary that wisdom have authority over reason. It is then that the soul sees that reason is not the light of true intelligence but is only the light of reason. For a longtime this vacillating intelligence had been mistakenly understood as truth.

Then the soul receives the true and firm intelligence that Paul describes here, an intelligence that does not vacillate. With the favor of this true intelligence, the soul discovers the ineffable mystery of the divine Father and the Son, as all science and wisdom of God is contained in his Word. God produces the eternal generation of the Word in souls. According to Paul, this intelligence is called the riches of assured understanding.

> For in him the whole fullness of deity dwells bodily, 10 and you have come to fullness in him, who is the head of every ruler and authority. (Col 2:9–10)

Jesus Christ has in him all the fullness of divinity, not as other human beings, but as what Paul calls the union of humanity with divinity. The Word is joined with human nature and this is the whole fullness of deity. Jesus Christ's grace flows out to humanity. Any person that is not united with Jesus Christ will not receive the influence of his grace.

> In him also you were circumcised with a spiritual circumcision, by putting off the body of the flesh in the circumcision of Christ; 12 when you were buried with him in baptism, you were also raised with him through faith in the power of God, who raised him from the dead. (Col 2:11–12)

Paul says that the true circumcision does not consist in the fleshly circumcision, or in exterior and excessive austerities done to the body. These do not give freedom to our soul. Jesus Christ accomplishes the true circumcision by changing who we are. We die to ourselves and all that we were in Adam. We lose ourselves, become hidden in God, and are raised with Jesus Christ. In the sacrament of baptism, (this is the mystical baptism of which he speaks here), Jesus Christ regenerates the soul. The soul is hidden and buried with him in God and resurrected with him. Through faith, we have entered into a new life. Jesus Christ accomplishes our death and resurrection.

> And when you were dead in trespasses and the uncircumcision of your flesh, God made you alive together with him, when he forgave us all our trespasses, 14 erasing the record that stood against us with its legal demands. He set this aside, nailing it to the cross. (Col 2:13–14)

The sin of death operates in all of us because of Adam's sin. Jesus Christ through his death and love brings resurrection to us. He forgives us our sins and we live in his grace, as he erases the record of sin that we received from the Father. We are acquitted by Christ's death on the cross. Divine justice has paid the debt of all that we have done. We received this debt because of sin and were condemned to death because of it. But we are freed from this debt and our condemnation is abolished.

There is a second death that happens to us after being freed from Adam's death and sin. We contract the new debt of propriety, the sin of trying to please other human beings, a sin which is in all of us. This debt must die. The design of God attracts our faith, to a greater or a lesser degree. Jesus Christ hides us within himself, paying our debts, as he applies the merits of his blood to us. We are resurrected by his grace, and he becomes our life.

> He disarmed the rulers and authorities and made a public example
> of them, triumphing over them in it. (Col 2:15)

My God! This beautiful Word! Jesus Christ dies to bring the souls to himself both in the particular and the church in general. He destroyed the principalities and powers of darkness, the cult which they worshipped. He destroyed corrupted nature under the domination of Adam. The principalities and powers were like royalty with their own spirit. Jesus Christ triumphed by his death, destroying this usurping authority. He exposed the demons. Through his power, he destroyed their stronghold that destroys us.

This is a general explanation, my God! The particular significance is beautiful! We have within us principalities and powers that imprison the soul, that are very powerful and proper. These powers want to be our master and propriety wants to corrupt us. Understanding is our gate, yet was corrupted by the spirit of propriety and self-glory. More corruption happened within us that destroys our will. Memory through self-interest and self-will falsely claims the will. Reasoning concerned with the self seizes the spirit and imprisons the true intelligence of the will.

The grace of God coming into the soul destroys these powers. Jesus Christ himself triumphs over the powers and principalities. And what does he do to triumph? He destroys all that gives the soul self-glorification: their glory, power, and self-reasoning. He exposes their corruption and their pride and leaves them nude, covered with shame and confusion, misery, and the baseness of ignominy. His power triumphs mightily throughout the world, bringing his opponents disgrace. This is the triumph of Jesus Christ over the life of Adam.

> Therefore do not let anyone condemn you in matters of food and drink or of observing festivals, new moons, or Sabbaths. 17 These are only a shadow of what is to come, but the substance belongs to Christ. (Col 2:16–17)

In Jesus Christ, souls triumph mightily over the powers that would completely destroy it and condemn it for certain exterior matters. These critical people are weak and they do not apply themselves to God. This is why they eat in particular ways and taste only outside things. In their matters of food and drink, they receive only death.

As Paul says, we must not be scandalized if people do not practice austerities, exercises, and practices. Some people value these practices very highly but these practices put people under pretense. This is not the shadow of the real presence of Jesus Christ.

This is the true mystical interpretation of this passage. The presence of Jesus Christ is proven and real, not imaginary and figurative.

> Do not let anyone disqualify you, insisting on self-abasement and worship of angels, dwelling on visions, puffed up without cause by a human way of thinking, 19 and not holding fast to the head from whom the whole body, nourished and held together by its ligament and sinews, grows with a growth that is from God. (Col 2:18–19)

Just and good worship includes simple and sincere devotion. The church approves and confesses that this worship is necessary for all Christians. However, many people join with superficial devotions that and do not participate in the essence of religion. They are attached only to images and figures resembling the original, yet are superstitious practices. These people condemn those not following these superstitions. Yet their practices torment them strangely and they become filled with error, illusion and lies.

These powerful people persecute those who remain faithful. They lose the prize of victory that Jesus Christ has won for us. They do this under the pretext of humility, saying that they are not worthy to be raised to a higher state. They pretend to stand in humiliation and penitence while practicing these superstitions. Clearly they are full of self-love and esteem themselves highly. They are full of the world's thinking. They become like fools and madmen, taking pride in their stubbornness. They pretend to have humility, yet they have no difficulty in condemning and fighting against others. They cry out against those living in the interior faith of Jesus Christ.

We must note their behavior. These people damage their souls and hurt the flock of Jesus Christ. They ignore Jesus Christ and influence others to do the same. They keep both their interior and exterior life for themselves. Rebelling against their destiny, they do not follow the intelligence of the Spirit but follow self-indulgence. Unstable, they act erratically. Filled with compulsion, they serve nothing. Instead, these people grow in their self-love and their propriety. How much they despise Christ!

If we receive Christ's inspiration and act according to it, if we believe and read the sacred Scriptures, we will grow and be nourished in God.

> If with Christ you died to the elemental spirits of the universe, why do you live as if you still belonged to the world? Why do you submit to regulations? 21 "Do not handle, Do not taste, Do not touch"? 22 All these regulations refer to things that perish with use; they are simply human commands and teachings. 23 These have indeed an appearance of wisdom in promoting self-imposed piety, humility, and severe treatment of the body, but they are of no value in checking self-indulgence. (Col 2:20–23)

Paul describes a state of propriety with activities based in self-love. The mortification of the flesh increases propriety, which is a sinful life lived for the approval of others. They follow superficial regulations. Paul says, if you have died to the elemental spirits of the universe and to self-directed activities, then the Christ changes us to live a spiritual life. This is why in the state of death we must no longer act out of self-love and propriety.

Contrary to these practices, Christ clothes the person in the death of self-activity because they hinder the spiritual life. God supports us while he transforms us, otherwise we could not bear this. God stops us from acting out of our self-indulgence.

My God! This wisdom of St. Paul is just and beautiful! If we listen to our holy Scriptures with care, we will not find this self-indulgent state, but a transcendent state. It is difficult for people practicing austerities to see that they are building their tomb with their own hands. Essentially they practice violence against themselves. They have left the will of God. They spend their time fighting against the understanding that these practices are destructive to them.

Instead, we must follow the wisdom of Paul. Do not do follow these severe practices, but live with simplicity in the state God gives us.

> So if you have been raised with Christ, seek the things that are
> above, where Christ is, seated at the right hand of God. 2 Set your
> minds on things that are above, not on things that are on earth.
> (Col 3:1–2)

The true and resurrected person sets her mind on the love from heaven and not on earthly matters. A faithful Christian lives in this world as if a stranger and values none of the world's pleasures. Also, she fears not the persecutions of human beings—the backbiting, the troubles, the insults—nothing touches the person. God alone is the person's occupation and love. But if one loves the things of this world, she will not be attached to goodness, love, honor, and faith. She lives in illusion and not in resurrection.

> So you have died, and your life is hidden with Christ in God. 4
> When Christ who is your life is revealed, then you also will be
> revealed with him in glory. (Col 3:3–4)

So when we are in the true death, the soul remains hidden with Jesus Christ in God. Jesus Christ leads the way and hides the soul for a longtime from the external world. Her hidden life frequently appears as nothing both to herself and others, but God possesses her life. She lives. Her life is like wheat growing from the seed, the life that springs from a seed hidden in the earth. It is not seen in the outside world until the right time of the manifestation of Jesus Christ.

Her life is like that of a baby bird living in a nest without care, worry, or concern. Her father and mother provide for everything she needs. She lives without thinking about her life. She enjoys singing and has beautiful feathers and a will. She has no concern about eating and drinking because it is given at the right time to her. She does not think about whether she will be strong, or how she will sing. None of this is her concern. She lives with strength until the manifestation of all that is.

The soul lives like this little bird by total abandon to the will of God. She lives without knowledge of her life, remaining *hidden with Jesus Christ in God* until the *manifestation of Jesus Christ*. This is like when the buried seed begins to grow above the ground and when the bird flies from the nest. Then Jesus Christ shows us the way to his Father and we are hidden with him in the Father who loves us and brings us life. Then the soul also appears with Christ in his glory. Then we are not in the glory of our self-love but in the glory of God.

> Put to death, therefore, whatever in you is earthly: fornication, im-
> purity, passion, evil desire, and greed (which is idolatry). (Col 3:5)

After Paul has spoken of the states of life hidden in God, he returns
again to the first elements of the Christian life, to show what is in the soul
before conversion. The state of conversion is the door through which we
must pass before we are introduced to more.

> Do not lie to one another, seeing that you have stripped off the old
> self with its practices 10 and have clothed yourselves with the new
> self, which is being renewed in knowledge according to the image
> of its creator. (Col 3:9–10)

After having spoken of the gross crimes that are destroyed in the first
conversion, Paul speaks here of the less common mistakes of lying and
hypocrisy that are stopped through the practice of virtues. Now that we
have become Christians, we still have a phoniness that formerly clothed us.
Simplicity, candor and innocence are the clothing of Jesus Christ. Therefore
we must take off the corrupted clothing of the old person with her dark
activities and falsehoods. Then Christ clothes us with the new and renewed
image of our creator and puts us in the simplicity and innocence of his creation. He renews our knowledge of God. He makes our intelligence simple
and free from the multiplicity of ways. This simplicity of the Spirit is the
state of innocence: the simple and unified human created in the image of
God.

> In that renewal there is no longer Greek and Jew, circumcised and
> uncircumcised, barbarian, Scythian, slave and free; but Christ is
> all and in all! (Col 3:11)

Now that the soul has arrived in God through Jesus Christ, she is no
longer slave or free. The soul no longer remains in self. Now Jesus Christ is
all in all for her and for others. Thus begins her union with God and union
with the neighbor.

> As God's chosen ones, holy and beloved, clothe yourselves with
> compassion, kindness, humility, meekness, and patience. 13 Bear
> with one another and, if anyone has a complaint against another,
> forgive each other; just as the Lord has forgiven you, so you also
> must forgive. 14 Above all, clothe yourselves with love, which binds
> everything together in perfect harmony. 15 And let the peace of
> Christ rule in your hearts, to which indeed you were called in the
> one body. And be thankful. (Col 3:12–15)

88

We must have love and tenderness for our neighbor, so sin may not enter. We must support our neighbors in their misery and not condemn them. We must show perfection toward our neighbors that we do not have within ourselves naturally. Yet if we are grounded in love and humility, then we support others naturally. We also excuse the faults of others.

This love that unites us to God and to our brothers and sisters links us to perfection. It produces peace in the heart and peace with our neighbor because we are united to God in love.

All the rest of this epistle is a series of instructions that I will not repeat, because I have already written about these ideas of Paul.

Bibliography

Anonymous. "Supplement to the Life of Madame Guyon." Translated by Nancy Carol James. In *The Pure Love of Madame Guyon*, 85–104. New York: University Press of America, 2014.

Barth, Marcus. *Ephesians*." Anchor Yale Bible 51. New Haven: Yale University Press, 1974.

Bedoyere, Michael de la. *The Archbishop and the Lady*. New York: Pantheon, 1956.

Bossuet, Jacques Benigne. *Quakerism a-la-mode, or A History of Quietism: Particularly that of the Lord Archbishop of Cambray and Madam Guyone*. London: Printed for J. Harris and A. Bell, 1698.

Bremond, Henri. *Apologie pour Fenelon*. Paris: Perrin, 1910.

Bruneau-Paine, Marie-Florine. *Women Mystics Confront the Modern World: Marie de l'Incarnation (1599–1672) and Madame Guyon (1648–1717)*. Albany, NY: SUNY Press, 1998.

Caussade, Jean Pierre de. *Abandonment to Divine Providence*. New York: Image, 1975.

———. *On Prayer: Spiritual Instructions on the Various States of Prayer according to the Doctrine of Bossuet, Bishop of Meaux*. Translated by Algar Thorold. London: Burns, Oates & Washbourne, 1931.

Conzemius, Viktor. "Quietism." In *Sacramentum Mundi*, edited by Karl Rahner et al., 5:169–72. New York: Herder & Herder, 1970.

Fénelon, Francois de Salignac de La Mothe. *The Archbishop of Cambray's Dissertation on Pure Love, with an Account of the Life and Writings of the Lady, for Whose Sake the Archbishop Was Banished from Court*. London: Thomson, 1750.

———. *The Complete Fénelon*. Brewster, MA: Paraclete, 2008.

———. *The Maxims of the Saints Explained, concerning the Interior Life*. Bordeaux, France: n.p., 1913.

Gondal, Marie-Louise. *Madame Guyon: un noveau visage*. Paris: Beauchesne 1989.

Gough, James. "Comparative View of the Lives of St. Teresa and M. Guion." In *The Life of Lady Guion*, 237–39, Bristol, UK: Farley, 1772.

———. "Life of Michael de Molinos and Progress of Quietism." In *The Life of Lady Guion*, 308–24. Bristol, UK: Farley, 1772.

Guyon, Jeanne de la Mothe. *Autobiography of Madame Guyon*. Vols. 1 and 2. Translated by Thomas Taylor Allen. London: Kegan Paul, Trench, Trubner, 1897.

Bibliography

————. *Les justifications de Mme J.-M.B. de La Mothe-Guyon, ecrites par elle-meme, avec un examen de la IXe et Xe conferences de Cassien touchant l'etat fixe d'oraison continuelle, par M. De* Fénelon. 3 vols. Cologne, 1720.

————. *Les livres de l'Ancien Testament de Notre-Seigneur Jésus-Christ avec des explications et réflexions qui regardent la vie intérieure.* 12 vols. Cologne, 1714–1715.

————. *Les livres du Nouveau Testament avec des explications et reflexions qui regardent la vie interieure.* Cologne: Poiret, 1713.

————. *Le Nouveau Testament de Notre-Seigneur Jésus-Christ avec des explications et réflexions qui regardent la vie intérieure.* 12 vols. Cologne: Poiret. 1714–1715.

————. *The Soul, Lover of God.* Translated by Nancy Carol James. New York: University Press of America, 2014.

————. *The Way of the Child Jesus: Our Model of Perfection.* Translated by Nancy Carol James. Arlington, VA: European Emblems, 2015.

Holcombe, William H. *Aphorisms of the New Life: With Illustrations and Confirmations from the New Testament, Fénelon, Madame Guyon, and Swedenborg.* Philadelphia: Claxton, 1883.

James, Nancy C. *The Apophatic Mysticism of Madame Guyon.* Ann Arbor, MI: UMI Dissertation Services, 1998.

————. *The Complete Madame Guyon.* Brewster, MA: Paraclete, 2011.

————. *I, Jeanne Guyon.* Jacksonville, FL: Christian, 2014.

————. *The Pure Love of Madame Guyon.* New York: University Press of America, 2007.

————. *Standing in the Whirlwind.* Cleveland: Pilgrim, 2005.

James, Nancy C., and Sharon D. Voros. *Bastille Witness: The Prison Autobiography of Madame Guyon.* New York: University Press of America, 2012.

James, William. *Varieties of Religious Experience.* New York: Collier, 1961.

Klaits, Joseph. *Servants of Satan: The Age of the Witch Hunts.* Bloomington: University of Indiana Press, 1986.

La Combe, Francois. *A Short Letter of Instruction, Shewing the Surest Way to Christian Perfection.* Translated by J. Gough. In *Life of Lady Guion*, 295–307. Bristol, UK: Farley, 1772.

Martin, Ralph P. *Ephesians, Colossians, and Philemon.* Atlanta: Knox, 1991.

Martyn, J. Louis. *Galatians.* New York: Doubleday, 1997.

Mudge, James. *Fénelon the Mystic.* Cincinnati: Jennings and Graham, 1906.

Poiret, Pierre. "The Theology of Emblems: Preface to the Emblems of Father Hugo and Madame Guyon." Translated by Nancy Carol James. In *The Soul, Lover of God*, by Madame Guyon, edited by Nancy Carol James, xxxiii–xl. New York: University Press of America, 2014.

Ramsay, Chevalier. "Life of Francis de Salignac de la Mothe Fénelon, Archbishop and Duke of Cambray." In *Life of Lady Guion*, 2:325–72. Bristol, UK: Farley, 1772.

Saint-Simon, Duc de. *Historical Memoirs of the Duc de Saint-Simon.* Vols. 1–2. Edited and translated by Lucy Norton. New York: McGraw-Hill, 1967.

Underhill, Evelyn. *Mysticism: A Study in the Nature and Development of Man's Spiritual Consciousness.* 12th ed. Cleveland: World, 1965.

Upham, Thomas C. *Life and Religions Opinions and Experience of Madame de la Mothe Guyon.* 2 vols. New York: Harper & Bros., 1847.

Ward, Patricia. *Experimental Theology in America: Madame Guyon, Fénelon and Their Readers.* Waco, Texas: Baylor University Press, 2009.

Wesley, John. *An Extract of the Life of Madame Guion.* London: Hawes, 1776.